Revolving Doors
Life and Love in the Hereafter

Skye Alexander

BookLocker

Trenton, Georgia

Print ISBN: 978-1-64719-832-9
Ebook ISBN: 978-1-64719-833-6

Published by BookLocker.com, Inc., Trenton, Georgia.

Printed on acid-free paper.

Library of Congress Cataloging in Publication Data
Alexander, Skye
Revolving Doors: Life and Love in the Hereafter by Skye Alexander
Library of Congress Control Number: 2021918597

BookLocker.com, Inc.
2022

First Edition

DEDICATION

To Ron, my co-author and partner in all things
here and hereafter, with love and gratitude

"You don't have a soul. You are a soul.
You have a body."
-- C. S. Lewis

ACKNOWLEDGMENTS

Heartfelt thanks to all of you who were there when I needed you: Sharon, Elise, Lyndsey, Anne, Harry, Claire, Leslie, Marilyn, Priscilla, Diane, Mary Lee, June, Nitia, and so many, many more who shepherded me through the dark times. Without you I would have been irrevocably lost. Thanks, too, to the staff of St. Luke's Hospital in San Antonio, Texas, for providing care and support during the most challenging ordeal of my life, and to the first responders at Tierra Linda's Volunteer Fire Department, especially George Turner.

AUTHOR'S NOTE

The events discussed in this book are as I remember them and as I recorded them over a period of several years. In Part One the names of the medical personnel have been changed. In the rest of the book, I've used only the first names of actual people who participated in this story, out of respect for their privacy.

TABLE OF CONTENTS

INTRODUCTION

We all have one thing in common: every one of us living here on earth will physically die. When you're young and healthy, you don't usually spend much time contemplating death or the hereafter. As you grow older, lose loved ones, or are diagnosed with a terminal condition, you're more likely to wonder what happens when you die. What's it like to be "dead"? Will part of you continue on after the demise of your corporeal self or is it "lights out" from there on out? Does a world beyond earth exist? Will you meet up with your loved ones again? Will you be reborn as somebody else in another time and place?

For millennia, mythology and religions have offered myriad views on these perplexing questions. In the last few decades especially, a plethora of best-selling books have been published that discuss the death experience and what lies ahead. Many of these books have been written by medical professionals, psychologists, and mediums. Others have been penned by people who've undergone near-death experiences and lived to tell the tale.

When my life partner, Ron Conroy, passed away unexpectedly in April 2013, I became intensely curious about life after death. The concepts of an afterlife and reincarnation weren't foreign to me. But I'd never before given them as much attention as I did now that the person who'd meant the most to me had suddenly vanished from the physical world.

My curiosity increased when he began talking to me from the "other side."

I'm not a doctor or a psychotherapist, nor am I a mystic, minister, or medium (even though much of the information contained in this book was conveyed to me in a manner similar to what mediums, channels, and psychics describe). I've never had a near-death experience. I'm just an ordinary woman who began hearing voices--and one beloved voice in particular--assuring me that everything was okay and encouraging me to delve deeper. I did.

I'm sharing with you what has been revealed to me because I firmly believe that each and every one of you can communicate with your loved ones in the afterlife if you choose to do so. I also believe these souls, spirits, whatever you choose to call them, really do want to communicate with you. They want you to realize that they're still alive and well, and that they still love you. They're not gone, they've merely slipped through a doorway into another "room" so to speak. You don't have to wait until you, too, have crossed over--you can talk with entities who no longer occupy physical bodies even while you still do. And you needn't be an "authority" to chat with them or maybe even see them.

Over the years, numerous studies have been done to determine the frequency of contact from the Great Beyond. In one study at Wayne State University in

Detroit, psychologist Robert Kastenbaum asked 140 people if they'd experienced this type of otherworldly communication; 45 percent answered *yes*. In another study done in Wales, Dr. W. D. Rees asked the same thing of 300 widows and widowers--and got a similar response: 47 percent said their departed spouses had contacted them. According to the University of Chicago's National Opinion Research Council, 78 percent of bereaved individuals said they saw their departed loved ones, 50 percent heard, and 18 percent talked with them.

In this book, I describe the so-called afterlife as my life partner, who is now in the spirit world, explained it to me and as I witnessed it. My experiences and what Ron shared with me may vary somewhat from those discussed by other people who have interacted with the worlds beyond earth and with the entities who occupy those worlds. Many levels of consciousness exist, more than we can even begin to imagine.

Discarnate beings experience the afterlife in their own individual ways, just as human beings experience our terrain uniquely. Souls perceive and interpret their environments according to their abilities--advanced souls will likely be able to convey more information than "beginner" souls. And, like people, souls have preferences. What one soul finds intriguing or valuable may not interest another.

Furthermore, human beings who study the afterlife may be more or less skilled at accessing, understanding, and interpreting the material they discover, and they'll approach it according to their personal belief systems. What I've described in this book is based on Ron's perspective, filtered through my understanding.

I say all this to suggest that the presence of different ideas about the afterlife doesn't mean one is right and another wrong, or that inconsistency discredits any of those ideas. They're simply different views, like those of the fabled blind men assessing the elephant.

However, I was surprised to discover how many similarities *do* exist between what Ron described to me and what many other writers, researchers, mediums, and NDEers have expressed. Undoubtedly, as people continue investigating the nature of the soul and what lies beyond earth, we'll gain information unbeknownst to us at present.

My intention in writing this book is not to convince you that an afterlife exists, or that an immortal part of us lives on after our physical bodies die. Many other researchers have presented extensive and compelling evidence to support these ideas. Organizations such as Forever Family Foundation, the Windbridge Institute, and the Afterlife Research and Educational Institution continue expanding our knowledge of consciousness through their work. I urge skeptics to read some of the many impressive books available about the afterlife. Listen to some of the fascinating radio and online programs presented by these and other organizations.

Please remember, a nonexistence of "proof" doesn't prove nonexistence.

If, by sharing my experience, I can bring a glimmer of hope to those who think you've "lost" a loved one, ease your fear and suffering, or encourage you to look more closely into the great mystery that has intrigued humankind since the beginning of time, then I will have accomplished my goal. My fondest wish is that you will come to know, as I have, that life never ends and love never dies.

PART ONE
Leaving the World We Know

"Being deeply loved by someone gives you strength,
while loving someone deeply gives you courage."
                                                        -- Lao Tzu

CHAPTER 1

At 2:22 on the afternoon of Good Friday, 2013, I answered an unexpected phone call from my longtime companion, Ron Conroy. Every afternoon at precisely 4:30, he telephoned to discuss plans for the evening, but rarely deviated from that routine.

Curious, I quipped, "To what do I owe the pleasure of this call?"

"I was just thinking about you," he answered.

His response surprised me. Much as I longed for verbal expressions of his affection, they were few and far between. Even after thirteen years together, he still introduced me as his "friend." Once, while he was traveling in Europe, he phoned to say he missed me, then added, "That's hard for me to say." Admitting he missed me meant he cared, and caring didn't compute with the image he held of himself as an independent, sophisticated, man of the world.

"I'm glad to know you think about me when I'm not around," I said.

"I do. A lot."

Those were the last words spoken to me by the man who'd been the center of my universe all these years. Two hours later he had a stroke that ended his life on earth.

• • •

When the phone rang again at 4:46, I almost didn't answer it. I didn't recognize the number on my Caller ID and I was hurrying to finish a proposal to send to my editor before calling it quits for the day. After the third ring, however, I clicked on.

A volunteer fireman who lived near Ron identified himself and said, "Ron's had a stroke. I responded to his 911 call. He's being airlifted to San Antonio."

I didn't panic. The child of an abusive alcoholic, I function best in a crisis. It's the little things that send me over the edge. I reminded myself that my mother had experienced numerous strokes, each causing a slight diminishment of her abilities. But Ron was so smart, so strong and healthy, a slight diminishment wouldn't be a bit deal. He was a tough guy, a former U.S. Air Force combat controller in Vietnam. He'd be okay.

After finding out which hospital the helicopter had flown Ron to and packing up a few things--including the latest edition of *National Geographic* and his reading glasses, which I fully believed he'd be able to use--I set out for San Antonio seventy miles south of our home.

Navigating San Antonio's rush-hour traffic is never an easy endeavor, especially on a holiday weekend, for a driving-averse, directionally challenged person like me. Even though I followed the MapQuest directions I'd printed out, I still got lost. Dusk settled in and I couldn't read the street signs. Now the panic I hadn't felt earlier gripped me. Where was I anyway? What if I couldn't find the hospital? I stopped at a convenience store to get directions, but the attendant spoke almost no English and I spoke even less Spanish.

It was 7:30 by the time I finally pulled into St. Luke's parking lot. At the front desk, a dark-haired woman with a pretty smile greeted me, consulted her computer, and told me Ron was still in surgery. I could go up to the Intensive Care Unit and wait.

I've only been in a few hospitals in my lifetime, once when I was six to have my tonsils removed, once shortly before my sister died, and twice more recently when Ron had his hips replaced. When he was fifteen, he'd broken a hip and his lower back in a football game. At that time, conventional medicine had no effective treatment for his injuries. Fifty years later, he underwent surgery to correct the damage and alleviate his constant pain.

In the ICU wing, a sign near a set of double doors instructed me to press a red button, and then stand in front of a video camera to await admittance. Another sign told me to disinfect my hands before entering. I pushed a container that squirted antibiotic gel on my palms and positioned myself in front of the camera. Several moments passed before someone buzzed me in.

Inside, I approached a desk made of pale wood and asked a woman with purple-framed glasses when Ron might get out of surgery.

"What is your relationship to Mr. Conroy?"

"Life partner, significant other, whatever it is we're called these days." The idea of referring to a sixty-nine-year-old man as a boyfriend seemed ridiculous.

The woman tapped her keyboard and consulted her computer monitor. "He's still in Recovery. He'll be brought to ICU when the doctor decides he's ready."

"May I wait here?" I asked, longing to remain one step closer to him and the source of information.

"Sure." She pointed down a long hallway. "Room number 7."

I entered a bleak room that smelled of disinfectant. A battery of mystifying machines stood like sentries, ready to be attached to Ron when he arrived. A sink, closet, small table, and a straight-backed wooden chair furnished the room. A whiteboard, a hand-sanitizing dispenser, and a container of blue plastic gloves hung on the walls. No feel-good pictures of rainbows or adorable children patting puppies, I noticed. From the window, I watched the streetlights over San Antonio and waited.

• • •

More than an hour passed before a team of medical personnel wheeled Ron, unconscious and strapped to a hospital bed, into Room 7 and began hooking up the array of machines. A nurse in blue scrubs adjusted a rack that held a plastic bag slowly filling with pinkish fluid and connected by a tube into his head. His beautiful, pure white hair--hair people stopped him in the supermarket to compliment--was stained dark red.

Another nurse examined the ventilator hose shoved down his throat to pump air into his lungs and keep his breathing steady. A third checked the IV needles in his hands and arms.

I stared at the bands that tied his wrists to the bed's guardrails.

"We had to restrain him," a nurse apologized. "He kept trying to pull out the IVs."

The nurse in blue recorded the numbers glowing on the various machines' displays, then left the room with the others in her wake.

I located the room's light switch and dimmed the overhead lamps. I'd never seen Ron so still. He was never still--even in sleep he twitched and rolled over every fifteen minutes or so, throughout the night.

While driving to the hospital, I'd imagined him sitting up in bed, impatient at this disruption in his schedule and ordering the hospital staff around like a drill sergeant commanding new inductees. Instead, he lay vulnerable, helpless, utterly devoid of the vitality, daring, and self-confidence that had brought him success in every area of his life.

Cautiously, I stepped up to the hospital bed and placed my hand on his wrist, just above the plastic ID bracelet. His pulse felt strong and steady. I stroked the hair on his forearm, the well-defined bicep, the curve of his shoulder that connected to a crooked collarbone he'd broken in a high school basketball game. A blue-and-tan johnnie covered him to his knees. White socks

13

with rubber soles encased his feet and calves. Shivering in the air-conditioned room, I touched each part of his body. Even without a blanket he seemed comfortably warm.

After a while, a tall, young Asian-American doctor entered the room. In a Texas accent, he introduced himself as Dr. Lee, the neurosurgeon who performed Ron's operation. I held out my hand and identified myself as Ron's medical representative.

"How is he? Tell me the truth."

The doctor motioned me to follow him out into the hallway. "There are two types of strokes," he began. "The more common involves a blockage that obstructs blood flow to the brain. The other type involves a hemorrhage in the brain. Mr. Conroy had a massive hemorrhage in the cerebellum area."

The surgeon held up his smartphone for me to look at and scrolled through a series of photos of Ron's brain. They showed a dark blotch about the size of my hand spreading across the lower back section, near the brain stem.

"I clamped off the ruptured cerebral artery," the doctor continued. "Now we're draining the excess fluid in his brain to reduce pressure."

"What does this mean?"

"He's in critical condition. Only about 20 percent of people who experience such an incident survive, and those who do frequently suffer a diminishment in their quality of life."

I gasped, unable to accept what he'd said. "How could this happen? He doesn't smoke, doesn't have high blood pressure. He eats right, exercises every day--he doesn't even take any medications. I can't remember him ever having a cold." But as I spoke, I wondered if Ron's type-A personality and his explosive Irish temper might be to blame.

"We believe it's congenital. In this portion of Mr. Conroy's brain, the arteries seemed malformed and the walls could have been abnormally weak. As he aged, the likelihood of a blood vessel bursting would have increased. If he never experienced any symptoms, though, no one would have thought to check it out." The surgeon consulted his phone again, and then showed me more pictures. "It's also possible that head trauma contributed to the problem."

As I stared at the photos, I considered Ron's car and motorcycle accidents, his numerous sports injuries. When he was young he'd been a world-class athlete, played semi-pro football, skied double-black diamonds, even competed for the Olympics. I recalled the studies of football players with brain damage and considered the injuries he'd incurred in his youth.

"He's strong and otherwise in excellent health," the doctor assured me. "He's got a good chance."

"If I talk to him, can he understand me?"

"He's heavily sedated at the moment, but patients often report being aware of what's going on around them even when they're in a coma." Dr. Lee patted my shoulder. "Go ahead, talk to him. Encourage him, give him hope. That's the best thing you can do for him right now."

After the surgeon left, I dampened a paper towel and gently washed Ron's face. Tears streamed down my cheeks and dripped onto his hospital gown. I gazed down at the man who just this morning had wrapped me in a full-body hug and kissed me warmly before I left for work.

Only 20 percent survive.

This morning while sitting at my computer an odd sense of dread had suddenly, inexplicably interrupted my concentration. The thought *could I go on living if Ron died* ran through my head. Of course I'd contemplated that possibility before, but always in a more detached way.

This time it felt different, immediate and poignant. Now I realized it had been a premonition.

"Ron, don't die. I can't bear to live without you." I struggled to keep my voice steady as I stroked his arm above the IV tube. "If you can hear me, please try to get better. The doctor said you have a good chance, and I know how strong-willed you are. You always accomplish whatever you set out to do. Please, please, don't give up."

Chapter 2

Machines beeped, groaned, chirped, buzzed, and sighed. Digital displays flashed arcane numbers and patterns. When a petite Latina RN with a ponytail, whose badge identified her as Sonia, came in to check Ron's vitals, I introduced myself and asked her to explain what the numbers meant.

Sonia smiled, shook my hand, and then pointed to a readout. "This monitors his heart rate. It's normal, seventy-two beats per minute. This one shows his respiratory rate. The ventilator is keeping it at eighteen breaths per minute. And this one measures his blood pressure. Right now it's holding steady at around 140 over 90. We're giving him medication to keep it under control to prevent any more stress on his brain."

"Thank you."

"Have you filed the paperwork?"

"What paperwork?"

"Giving you legal authority to make decisions about his medical care."

I shook my head. "The paperwork is at home."

"We're going to need that information as soon as possible."

"But it's a three-hour round-trip. And I don't want to leave him like this."

"You can take care of it tomorrow." Sonia made several notations on her clipboard, then asked, "Did you get anything to eat? The cafeteria closes soon."

"I'm not hungry." I could use a drink, though, I thought. Too bad hospitals don't have bars.

"Okay, I'll be here all night and I'll check in on him at least once every half-hour. If you need me, just ask at the desk and someone will page me." She smiled in what was probably meant to be a reassuring way, but my confidence had diminished significantly since Dr. Lee's visit. "He's a handsome man."

"Yes, he is," I agreed.

Even at sixty-nine, Ron still turned heads when he entered a room. One of his friends had nicknamed him "Hollywood" because he had a movie star's good looks and charisma. People who saw him often thought he was someone famous.

After Sonia left, I assured him, "Just in case you're worried, your face looks fine. No drooping or paralysis. But somebody in ER gave you a really bad haircut."

For the next hour, I stood beside Ron's bed and told him how much I loved him, how important he was to me, how desperately I needed him. When the fear and sadness overwhelmed me, I found an empty room in the ICU wing where I could sob privately. He hated to see me cry, but I couldn't stop the tears; the best I could do was try not to break down in his presence.

• • •

From the window in Ron's ICU room, I watched the amber-colored lights along Interstate 410 flash their messages. Inside St. Luke's, the machines keeping him alive flashed their own messages. Every half-hour, as promised, Sonia consulted those machines. Once she emptied Ron's urine-collecting bag; another time she cleared the plastic sack into which his brain fluids drained. When the X-ray technicians showed up near midnight to scan his chest, I touched his arm and explained what was happening.

I hadn't felt hungry earlier in the evening, but now my stomach growled loudly. Leaving the technicians to their business, I exited the ICU wing, took the elevator down to the hospital's first floor, and began exploring. Outside the now-closed cafeteria I found a vending machine and slid quarters into it. A package of mixed nuts and a chocolate bar dropped into the receptacle.

On the way back to the elevator, I saw a sign for St. Luke's chapel. On impulse, I followed the arrows to a small sanctuary with a dozen or so pews and potted lily plants arranged around the altar. Easter weekend, I recalled as I entered the empty chapel.

Although I had no religious affiliation and Ron had rejected the Catholic Church long before I met him, I took a seat. Here in this silent retreat, I petitioned every deity I could think of to let Ron live. Tears streamed down my cheeks. I sobbed uncontrollably, my body shuddering. All the anguish I'd been trying to contain suddenly gushed out, and I rocked back and forth like a mental patient, hugging myself as if to keep my heart from exploding.

I had no idea how long I'd been sitting there when a short, brown-skinned woman wearing a sari entered the chapel and took a seat across the aisle. She bowed her head, and, I assumed, prayed to her own gods. A woman just like me, awash in fear, grief, and desperate hope.

I wiped my tears, stood, and left the chapel. After its subdued illumination, the glaring fluorescent lights in the hospital's corridors hurt my swollen eyes. Only a few staff and an occasional visitor moved about in the stark environment. I disinfected my hands again before entering the ICU, and stood in front of the camera until someone buzzed me in.

Ron lay just as I'd left him. The ventilator filled the room with its rhythmic rasping, forcing him to breathe. Lights glowed on the digital displays. Standing by the side of his narrow hospital bed, I laid my hand on his arm.

"Everything's going to be all right," I said with a confidence I didn't feel.

• • •

Throughout the night nurses, doctors, and technicians of all sorts came and went. They poked and prodded, shone penlights in Ron's eyes, checked the machines, wheeled in more machines, jotted down information, and occasionally offered words of encouragement. I tried to sleep, but found it impossible sitting up in the wooden chair with the barrage of noises emitted by the equipment.

"Can you turn down the volume on the machines?" I asked Sonia.

The RN answered, "We have to be able to hear if something goes wrong."

"Could you bring him some earplugs? He has very sensitive hearing."

"We want him to be able to hear us and respond."

After the nurse left, I said to Ron, "I'm so sorry, darlin'. I know you hate all this. I wish I could make things better for you. I feel so helpless. I wish you could talk and tell me what to do."

I slipped my fingers into his nearly closed hand and felt him squeeze them ever so slightly.

"Oh! Can you hear me? Do you know I'm here?"

I felt pressure on my fingers again.

A flicker of hope leapt in my chest. "Good, at least we can communicate. How about I ask questions and you squeeze my hand if the answer is yes?"

He squeezed.

"Are you in pain?"

Yes.

"Your head?"

Yes.

"Is it really bad?"

No.

"Anywhere else?"

No.

"I wish I could take that damned tube out of your throat. That's got to be uncomfortable."

Yes.

"Ron, I love you so much. Please get well."

Yes.

Shortly before three in the morning Sonia, followed by an aide, came in carrying a dishpan full of plastic bottles and towels.

"He's conscious," I told her. "He can understand me and respond by squeezing my hand."

"That's good news." Sonia took Ron's hand. "Mr. Conroy, can you hear me? Squeeze my hand if you can . . . good. We're going to give you a bath, okay? We'll try to be gentle . . . good."

"Getting a sponge bath from two pretty women will be the high point of his day."

"Would you step outside so we have more room to work?" Sonia asked.

I touched his cheek lightly and told him, "I'll be back in a bit."

CHAPTER 3

While I wandered the halls of St. Luke's, my mind flashed back to the first time I met Ron, on Memorial Day weekend, thirteen years ago. I was driving home from the train station in Rockport, Massachusetts after saying goodbye a man I'd dated briefly. About two miles from my house, I asked aloud, "Okay, Goddess, what have you got for me now?"

As I turned into my driveway and climbed out of my Honda, I heard someone call my name. I turned and watched a man on a bicycle pedal up to me. He pulled off his helmet and shook out his snowy hair, then removed his sunglasses and flashed me a neon-blue gaze. I appraised him quickly, from his neatly trimmed beard down to his muscular calves, and I liked what I saw.

He held out his hand. "I'm Ron Conroy."

The name rang a bell. I recalled a friend telling me about a man she'd known some twenty-odd years ago who'd recently returned to Cape Ann after years of living in Hawaii. My *yenta* friend thought I should meet him. I shook his hand and asked if he'd like a glass of water, iced tea, or something stronger.

For the next hour we sat on my deck and swapped information. We talked about Hawaii, his job as an air traffic controller, my writing, the places we'd traveled, people we knew, wine, movies, books. We both liked Cormac McCarthy and John Fowles. At the end of our conversation, he suggested having dinner together that evening. He liked to cook and would bring everything to my house. An offer I couldn't refuse.

• • •

When I returned to the ICU, I saw Sonia sitting just outside Room 7, squinting at a computer monitor and writing notes in a file.

"How's he doing?"

"Holding his own. If the doctor thinks he's ready, we'll take him off the ventilator in the morning and see if he can breathe by himself."

"That's terrific." Thank you, thank you, I silently said to the deities I'd asked for help.

"He's not out of the woods yet," Sonia cautioned, "but so far so good."

I took up my vigil beside Ron's bed and held his hand. "I'm back, darlin'." I noticed someone had removed the restraints that had tied his arms to the bed rails. "Oh, good, they took off those handcuffs and washed your hair. Feel better after your bath?"

He squeezed my fingers.

"Did you hear the nurse? If the doctor says it's okay, they'll take that awful tube out of your throat soon. I know you'll feel better then."

Yes.

"I love you, Ron."

24

He squeezed my fingers. *I love you too.*

I sat in the uncomfortable wooden chair, slipped off my sandals, and propped my bare feet up on his bed, touching my toes to his. I ate the last of my chocolate bar while watching his chest rise and fall. When he shifted his feet and bent one knee slightly, I jumped up and took his hand.

"Are you okay? Comfortable--at least as much as possible under the circumstances?"

Yes.

"I wish I could curl up next to you, but you've got so many tubes sticking out of you, I'm afraid I might knock something loose. Maybe tomorrow."

Yes.

I kissed his cheek. "I love you."

Every hour, pulmonary nurses, X-ray technicians, and other personnel bearing the tools of their trade wandered in, making it impossible for either of us to get any sleep. In between, I sat at his bedside, caressing his arm or leg, telling him I loved him.

"Even now you're the handsomest, sexiest, most exciting man in the world," I said.

I could almost hear him laugh. "It's true," I insisted, countering the imagined rebuff. "Don't worry, darlin', you won't end up in a wheelchair dragging an oxygen tank behind you. You're going to be okay."

At around seven the sky began to pale as sunrise approached. Sonia came in accompanied by a tall, big-boned nurse with cropped blond hair and very pink cheeks.

"I'm leaving now," the RN said. "Margot here will be taking care of Mr. Conroy during the day shift. I'll be back around 6:30 this evening. The doctors usually start their morning rounds at eight, so if you're hungry this would be a good time to get a bite at the cafeteria."

"Good idea," I said.

"Are you his . . . daughter?" Margot asked.

"I hope he didn't hear that," I answered. "No, I guess you could call me his companion. He's only six years older than me, but obviously he's not looking his best at the moment."

As Margot started her routine check, I told Ron I was going downstairs to get some breakfast. I rode the elevator to the ground level, but before heading for the cafeteria I visited the chapel. Morning light streamed in through the stained-glass windows, casting colorful patterns around the intimate space. No other praying hopefuls occupied pews at this early hour, and I took a seat in the back row.

Folding my hands in my lap, I whispered, "Thank you. Please give him the strength, determination, and patience to get well. He doesn't like it when things don't go his way. And if Dr. Lee is right, even if Ron survives . . . he might never be 100 percent again . . ." My voice cracked and tears sprang into my eyes.

I began sobbing, quietly at first, then louder, my chest heaving as I gave in to my anxiety in the quiet sanctuary. Ron's greatest fear was being physically incapacitated, reliant on others to tend to his most basic needs. Fiercely independent, a world traveler, a man who'd controlled the lives of millions of people throughout his distinguished career, he couldn't have stood to be diminished.

When my tears finally subsided, I wiped my eyes. "I guess I'm the one who needs strength, determination, and patience. Please help us both."

Hospital staff preparing for the day's work crowded the cafeteria. They chatted easily among themselves, like employees at any company. How can they do it? I wondered. How can they remain sane? I noticed an elderly woman sitting alone at a table, poking at her breakfast, but eating little. The woman's eyes were as red and swollen as I assumed mine must be. How can *we* stay sane?

I poured myself a large coffee. A server scooped over-cooked scrambled eggs and greasy bacon onto my plate. I paid the cashier and, for a moment, considered going to sit with the elderly woman, but I couldn't handle another person's pain right now. It was all I could do to keep from screaming.

When I returned to the ICU wing a hubbub of busy professionals greeted me in Room 7. Margot adjusted a lever on the machine that drained Ron's brain fluid. An aide carried out his urine bag. A pulmonary nurse checked his ventilator. Although I was grateful for its efficiency, I'd come to loathe the intrusive machine's omnipresent wheezing. How I longed to hear Ron's own deep, steady breathing again.

I touched his arm. In what I hoped was a chipper voice, I said, "Howdy, darlin'. I'm back. Did you miss me?"

Margot glanced at the digital displays, recorded his vitals--which were still normal--and smiled. Dimples dented the blond nurse's rosy cheeks. She fluffed some pillows under Ron's back and hips to make him more comfortable, then peeled off her blue plastic gloves and gave me a thumbs-up sign.

At quarter past eight the pulmonary specialist, a striking, silver-haired man about my age, arrived and introduced himself as Dr. Wasserman.

I shook his hand and said, "I'm Skye Alexander, his medical representative."

After skimming through Ron's folder, examining the patient, and conferring with Margot, the doctor told me, "I'm going to check on him again in a couple hours. If all continues to go well, we'll take him off the ventilator."

"That would be wonderful."

"I won't tell you not to worry, but he has a fighting chance. A lot is up to him. I firmly believe a patient's will to live is a major factor in his recovery. We see miracles here all the time. Don't give up."

"Never."

CHAPTER 4

As morning's pink and gold tendrils slid across the blue-gray sky, I retreated to one of the empty ICU rooms and started phoning friends.

"How can that be?" each of them wondered aloud. "Ron was so strong, so healthy."

I explained what the neurosurgeon had said. "His doctor believes it's congenital. Nothing he could have known about or prepared for."

I couldn't help thinking about Ron's identical twin brother Terry who'd died of a brain tumor twenty-five years ago. The tumor had grown in his brainstem, the area beside the cerebellum where Ron's hemorrhage occurred. Was Terry's death related to a congenital weakness too, or simply a coincidence?

It was too early yet to call Ron's California friends Sharon and Elise. Both retired nurses, they'd visited us in Texas at Christmas. Sharon had been Terry's girlfriend back in the seventies. Elise's identical twin sister had died years earlier, which cemented her relationship with Ron in a way that only twins could understand.

I returned to Ron's room and read for the next few hours, listening to the sound of his steady breathing. With each breath he took I felt more confident.

Occasionally I heard him snore and was glad he could sleep. Dr. Lee stopped in briefly to visit his patient and smiled at me.

"How is he?" I asked.

"Holding his own."

When Margot checked in, she told me, "We're going to give him some food now."

"He likes his steak medium rare."

"Sorry, he'll be on a liquid diet for a while." She hung a plastic bag filled with brownish gunk alongside the other bags of medications, nutrients, and fluids flowing into Ron's body.

Finally, Dr. Wasserman, followed by a dozen or so medical students, approached Room 7. Leaving the group outside, he entered and said hello. While he checked Ron's breathing, I anxiously held my own breath. The pulmonologist noted the readouts on the equipment, consulted paperwork, and jotted down some additional information.

"Okay, let's see if he can manage on his own. We'll leave the ventilator tube in place, though, in case we need to use it again."

"That's great news."

"Keep the faith," he said and rejoined the cluster of students in the hall.

A few minutes later, a man wearing green scrubs entered the room and turned off the machine. Without its constant groaning the room seemed eerily quiet. I held Ron's hand, noticing that it had swollen overnight.

The skin was stretched tight over knuckles scarred from numerous barroom brawls. I watched his chest rise and fall with each unaided breath, silently willing him to continue.

"I love you."

He squeezed my fingers.

"You're doing fine. You've got to keep breathing. I know you can do it."

Yes.

"Good. Are you reasonably comfortable?"

Yes.

"Anything I can do for you?"

No.

I kissed his cheek, where a prickle of hairs had already begun to grow.

"I've got to go home to get the papers that give me the right to make medical decisions for you, until you can make them yourself. I'll be back as soon as I can. Hang in there darlin'."

He squeezed my fingers again.

On the way to the car, I detoured into the hospital's chapel. A new arrangement of white carnations and pink stargazer lilies sat on the altar. I inhaled their heady fragrance and thanked the deities for Ron's improvement.

• • •

I hadn't fully realized the depth of my fatigue until I stepped out of the shower. I wrapped myself in my bathrobe and lay down for a nap. When my doorbell jarred me awake, I was surprised to see that the sky had deep turned purple and the moon hung low on the horizon. Two friends stood on the front porch, bearing Chinese take-out and a bottle of wine.

Priscilla took plates, glasses, and silverware from my kitchen cabinets. Marilyn scooped fried egg rolls, moo shi pork, shrimp with snow peas, and rice onto the plates. I was glad to let them take charge.

"Sit. Eat," Marilyn ordered, arranging dinner on my antique oak dining table.

Priscilla dipped her egg roll into sweet-and-sour sauce. "Fill us in."

I explained as much as I understood. "Everyone seems to think he has a good chance of pulling through. Still, only one person in five survives a stroke like this."

"If anyone can, it's Ron," Priscilla said.

"Yes, but those who do . . . how'd the doctor put it . . . 'often suffer a diminishment in their quality of life.' "

"What exactly does that mean?" Marilyn asked.

"I'm not sure. I guess it varies from person to person." I thought of Ron being nourished with foul-looking goo pumped through a feeding tube. "What if he comes out of it paralyzed? Being helpless is his worst fear. He's always sworn he'll never end up a cripple."

Priscilla patted my hand. "I think you're jumping to conclusions. You said he was improving."

"Yes, but if he thought that was going to happen, he'd rather die." I tucked a lock of blond hair behind my ear and gazed out the window, my eyes filling with tears. "Can you imagine Ron in a wheelchair?"

"No, but let's not go there yet."

Throughout the evening, my friends' support and encouragement gradually lifted my spirits and gave me hope. Maybe things weren't as bleak as they seemed. But shortly after they'd said their goodbyes, my cell phone chimed. I grabbed it and glanced at the Caller ID: St. Luke's Hospital.

"Ms. Alexander?"

"Yes."

"This is Sonia Ortez at St. Luke's Hospital ICU. I need your permission to have a central line inserted into Mr. Conroy's heart."

My own heart skipped a beat. "What is it and why does he need it?"

"It's a catheter surgically inserted into his upper chest that will enable us to give him medications faster and more directly. His extremities have swollen due to his immobility. This way we won't have to restart IVs in his arms and hands if they become clogged," Sonia explained. "There is a risk of infection, however."

"How big a risk?"

"Not very. The benefits, we believe, outweigh the potential risks."

"All right then, do it."

"Would you please repeat this to my colleague, so there's no doubt?"

"Okay," I agreed, my anxiety level rising. Directly into his heart. Risk of infection.

Although Sonia seemed almost matter-of-fact, a late-night phone call that required my authorization and verification to protect the hospital against possible reprisals raised a big red flag. I didn't understand the details, but sensed this wasn't just a simple, everyday procedure.

I repeated my go-ahead to another nurse, and then Sonia came back on the line.

"How is he, Sonia?"

"We had to put him back on the ventilator."

"Why? He was breathing fine when I left."

"Maybe it was just a little too soon. In the morning he may be ready to try again."

I considered driving to San Antonio immediately, but realized I was too exhausted and had drunk too much wine to safely make the trip. Damn it, I swore mentally, angry at myself for not being there when Ron needed me. At a situation that had deteriorated since I'd left the hospital this afternoon. I wished I could dematerialize and rematerialize in Room 7. He'd improved while I was there--did my presence influence his healing? No, that was giving myself too much credit.

"Sonia," I said, my voice quivering. "Please do whatever you have to do to keep him alive. I can't survive without him."

CHAPTER 5

One night, about four months into our relationship, Ron woke me up, conversing with his long-deceased brother.

"Who are you talking to?" I asked.

"Terry. He was here. I can't believe you didn't see him."

Someone else might have thought he was dreaming and told him to go back to sleep. But I'm a woo-woo kind of girl. I do astrology charts and tarot readings, I write books about metaphysical stuff, and I've had my share of paranormal experiences. Even though I didn't see Terry that night, I fully believed Ron had.

Like many identical twins, they could read each other's minds. They finished one another's sentences, answered each other's unspoken questions. As little kids they sat side by side on the kitchen floor building skyscrapers and fortresses with their matching erector sets. If one twin couldn't locate the piece he needed, the other instinctively handed it to him. As teens on the gridiron or basketball court, Ron knew where his brother would be before he got there; he could throw the ball to a spot, confident Terry would arrive just in time to catch it.

Nothing could fill the gap left by Terry's death. When you're born an identical twin, Ron explained to me, you grow up thinking of yourself as half of a pair. Like socks or gloves, one is superfluous without the other. A psychologist might insist he only imagined his brother's visits, or that he was in denial or attempting to compensate for the loss. But I believe our spirits live on after our physical bodies die, so I didn't doubt Ron and Terry could still communicate. I only wished I knew what they were saying.

• • •

No choir sung in St. Luke's chapel on Easter morning. No minister preached the Good News. I slipped into Room 7 of the ICU and stood beside Ron's bed. The ventilator wheezed and I checked his vitals on the monitors, noting that his blood pressure had ratcheted up ten points; the others read normal. I leaned down to kiss his cheek and grasped his hand.

"Darlin' I'm here," I said. "I'm so sorry I had to leave you." Although his swollen fingers could no longer squeeze my hand and his eyes remained shut, I knew he was awake. "I got in touch with Sharon and Elise and they're flying in tomorrow. I also talked to a lot of your other friends--they're all rooting for you."

When Margot entered the room to check on her patient I asked, "What happened? He was breathing fine yesterday afternoon."

The nurse shrugged. "Healing sometimes follows an up and down route. Dr. Wasserman will stop by soon--you can discuss it with him."

"Thanks," I said, trying to rein in my fear.

After Margot finished her ministrations and left, I stood beside Ron's bed studying the shape of his lips, his white hair with the big shaved patch on one side, his muscular arms now swollen with edema, trying to commit every mole and scar and wrinkle to memory. Gently I traced his fingernails--broader at the tips than at the cuticles, the sign of a risk-taker, or so I'd read somewhere. Now he faced the greatest challenge in his sixty-nine years.

"Have you been talking to Terry?" I asked.

He moved his foot--the only gesture left to him--to signal *yes*.

"Tell him you're not ready to cross over. You and he were together for forty-four years, I've only been with you for thirteen."

I sensed him chuckle inwardly, but I felt no mirth, only fear. It seemed the twins were conspiring against me, and I knew I couldn't compete. In their closed circle of two, I was an outsider. I kissed Ron's cheek and told him I loved him, just as the biggest, blackest man I'd ever seen rolled a reclining chair upholstered in turquoise vinyl into Room 7.

"I saw you trying to sleep in that schoolhouse chair the other night and figured you might could use this."

The man showed me how to adjust the recliner's back and lock its wheels.

"Thank you," I said, touched by his consideration.

"No problem. Guard it, though. We only have a few and they tend to get 'appropriated' if you leave them unattended."

"Got it."

"Let me know if you need anything else. My name's Sugar Ray."

"After the boxer? You look more like a linebacker to me."

He flashed a mouthful of white teeth. "My mama was a big boxing fan. I guess she didn't know when I was born that I'd grow this big."

The temperature in the hospital's ICU was kept uncomfortably cool to help prevent the growth of germs, so I'd brought a quilt from home. I unfolded it and spread it over the recliner, claiming my territory. Then I settled in with a book, my feet propped on Ron's bed, and waited for whatever came next.

About an hour later Dr. Wasserman arrived, this time without his entourage. After greeting me, he examined Ron and checked the ventilator.

"He was getting better. Why did he backslide?"

"I don't know the answer to that, but it happens. Tomorrow he may rally and we can try again."

I couldn't pinpoint why, but I felt he wasn't telling me everything. "I brought the paperwork," I said.

"Good, take it to the nurses' station. They'll make photocopies and put them in Mr. Conroy's file." Dr. Wasserman laid his hand on my shoulder. "I know this is hard for you, but you need to be strong now. We're doing everything we can for him. He needs you to do everything you can too."

After the doctor left, I handed the legal documents to a nurse to copy. Then I took the elevator downstairs to the security office to collect Ron's wallet. Now that I was officially on record as his medical representative, they could release his personal property to me.

I swung by the cafeteria for a cup of take-out coffee and made a quick visit to the empty chapel. Even though my spiritual beliefs would have raised most ministers' eyebrows, I drew a tiny bit of comfort from the hushed sanctuary with its stained-glass windows and flowers. In the hubbub that never stopped at St. Luke's, this quiet little corner gave me a place to escape and momentarily let down my guard.

On the way back to ICU, I dropped by the ladies' room. While I washed my hands, the woman who stared back at me from the mirror looked ten years older than the one who'd faced me only two days ago. Her fair skin resembled old parchment and her blond hair had lost all its shine. Purple half-moons hung beneath her blue eyes.

I pulled my hair away from my face, then let it fall back loose at my shoulders. What difference did my appearance make? Ron couldn't see me anyway--he hadn't opened his eyes today except when a nurse peeled back his lids and shone a penlight into them.

CHAPTER 6

Sharon's phone call woke me.

"We're in the lobby. On our way up."

"Thanks for coming," I said. "I'm glad you're here."

A few minutes later, Ron's longtime friends strode into Room 7. They hugged me quickly, then pushed past me to his bedside. Knowing they'd been in his life for decades and that they were both retired RNs gave me a tiny bit of comfort. They could talk to the doctors in their arcane language, help guide Ron's progress, and tell me what to do.

Sharon's pretty face revealed nothing, but worry lines etched Elise's tough-girl expression. It only took them a few moments to assess the situation.

"He's worse than I imagined," Elise said. "Pull the plug, now."

I felt as though she'd punched me in the stomach. I'd hoped his friend would say things weren't as bleak as they seemed, that she'd seen patients recover from worse.

"He can hear and understand you," I reminded her. "His doctor said they see miracles here every day. He could pull through."

Sharon turned away and gazed out the window overlooking the city of San Antonio. Elise's dark eyes brimmed with tears.

I left Room 7, giving them some time alone with Ron. In the hallway, I spotted the neurosurgeon, Dr. Lee, and called out to him. Elise may have witnessed plenty of illness and trauma in her career as an RN, however, I wasn't ready to accept her assessment. The tall, young doctor held out his hand. I shook it weakly and told him what Elise had surmised.

"You gave me hope before," I said. "Now I need to know the truth."

After a long pause, Dr. Lee answered, "The part of his brain affected by the stroke plays a key role in his motor control, coordination, and balance. He may never walk or talk again."

I gasped, then clamped my hand over my mouth to keep from crying out.

"He might have to be on oxygen," the surgeon continued. "It's possible he'll need a feeding tube. He could experience loss of cognitive function."

"Might? Possible? What are the odds he'll beat this?"

"Not good."

I shook my head, not willing to believe what I'd heard. "No, that can't be."

"Of course, each patient is different. I'm not writing him off. Sometimes people come out of these situations and go on to live for years. I've seen patients I thought were goners emerge, in time. Each patient is different.

But you need to understand the probabilities and be willing to accept them." He paused, as if gauging my ability to comprehend. "We can keep him alive for as long as you choose. You have to decide what's best for him."

• • •

I took the elevator down to the first floor. Avoiding the chapel, I wandered instead into the hospital gift shop to kill time. If there was a Goddess, she hadn't heard my pleas--or had ignored them.

After letting an hour pass, I returned to the ICU. Sharon sat in the turquoise recliner, recollecting the old days, laughing and crying simultaneously. Elise stood on the other side of Ron's bed, her hand on his arm. I leaned against the sink, and noticed his plastic identification band and the silver-link bracelet he always wore lying on the counter. My *yenta* friend, the one who'd introduced us, made the bracelet for him more than two decades ago. Until now, he'd never taken it off. I picked it up and turned it over in my hands.

"I took them off, they were too tight," Elise said. "Give me the silver one."

I did, and she fastened the bracelet around my wrist, shortening the links to keep it from sliding off. I approached his bed and stroked his arm, now bare except for the IV.

"I'm back, darlin'," I said, trying to hide my fear. "Hope y'all had a good visit."

"Did you think any more about what I said?" Elise asked.

"I don't want to discuss it in front of him."

"Why not? He has a right to know what's going on."

"I talked to his neurosurgeon . . ."

"And the doc agreed with me, right?"

Struggling to hold back my tears, I answered, "Nothing's definite, but he wasn't very encouraging."

"I've known Ron more than forty years," Sharon said, gently. "I know he'd never want to live like this. You know that too."

"Ask him then," I countered. "He'll move his foot to answer yes or no."

A raw sadness gripped me as I watched the strong, vibrant, independent man I'd loved so long execute the only voluntary movement left to him.

"Okay," Sharon said. "Bend your toes if the answer is yes."

Elise plucked a Kleenex from a box near his bed and blew her nose, then tossed the crumpled tissue in the trash. She brushed his shoulder gently with her fingertips.

"Ron, you know we love you very much. You know we don't want to lose you, but we want what's best for you." Sharon glanced at me for validation before asking, "Do you want us to take you off life support?"

Ron bent his toes.

• • •

"I need a drink and a steak," Elise said. "And we need to talk."

We took a taxi to a nearby restaurant, where we ordered rib-eye steaks and a good bottle of California cabernet sauvignon. Sharon raised her glass. "To Ron, my dear friend."

"To Ron, the love of my life," I answered.

We'd finished the first glass of wine by the time the waiter brought our dinners. He refilled our glasses, and we toasted again.

Elise cut into her perfectly prepared steak. "Damn that's good."

"Texans do know how to grill steak," I said.

After a few bites, Sharon laid down her silverware and speared me with her eyes. "We have to be on the same page about this."

I looked down at my plate and twisted my napkin in my lap. Everything seemed to be happening too fast, and nothing felt real. Only a few days ago, Ron had been his usual energetic, take-charge self. Now we were talking over a delicious dinner about consigning him to death.

"I know it's your decision," Elise continued. "He trusted you with his life and death. You were probably the only woman he ever trusted."

I nodded, unable to speak.

"The longer he remains in this vegetative state, the worse his chances are of recovery," Sharon pointed out.

"Have you considered what his life might be like if he survives? What *your* life might be like?"

I thought about the nurses giving him sponge baths and emptying his urine bag. For me, performing such intimate daily rituals would be a labor of love, but for him a gross humiliation.

"Skye, get real," Elise said. "He is not going to walk out of that hospital room. He may never be able to do more than wiggle his toes."

"My heart doesn't want to accept that."

"If you really love him you have to set him free," Sharon said.

I wiped my tears with my napkin and tried to hold myself together. "I do."

• • •

After the cab dropped Sharon and Elise off at their hotel, I returned to St. Luke's and went to an empty room in the ICU to phone my friend Lyndsey in Massachusetts. After relating Elise's take on Ron's condition, I said, "We promised we'd never let each other end up incapacitated or in a nursing home. He used to say, 'When I can't wipe my own butt, I'm out of here.' "

"Skye, people do recover from strokes and go on to live normal lives."

"Except he doesn't want to live."

"What do you mean?"

"He's suffered from depression since his brother died twenty-five years ago. But being the tough guy he is, he refused to get treatment. Usually he expressed the depression as anger. He tried to put a good face on things, for me and other people," I continued. "But for the last year, he's been talking about shooting himself."

"That doesn't make any sense. He had everything anyone could want--success, money, a woman who loved him, friends, a beautiful home . . ."

"But if you're not at peace with yourself all those things most of us value don't matter."

"I didn't realize he felt that way."

"I guess I didn't want to believe it."

CHAPTER 7

Throughout the night, I stood by Ron's bedside and talked to him. This was my last chance to express all the things I'd never said before.

"I hope you know how much you mean to me and how grateful I am for having had the opportunity to spend all these years with you. You were always so strong and brave and sure of yourself, and I've always felt so confused and scared and inadequate. You took care of me and kept me safe. You were my rock, my port in the storm, my knight in shining armor. You were all I ever wanted."

Choking back sobs, I continued, "No man ever showed much interest in me before. You encouraged me and helped me find a direction in life. You made me feel beautiful and worthy and loved. You could've had any woman you wanted, but for some reason you chose me--I still don't know why, but I'm glad you did."

His breath grew harsh and irregular. Tears leaked from the corners of his eyes. I blotted them with a tissue and glanced at the monitor. His blood pressure had ratcheted up several points.

"I'm sorry, I didn't mean to upset you," I said. "Do you want me to get the nurse?"

No.

"Okay, then I'll be quiet. Try to rest. I love you."

I curled up in the recliner, wrapped myself in the quilt, and cried as quietly as I could. After a while, Ron's breathing deepened and he slept. I dozed too and dreamed about his twin brother. In the dream I shouted at Terry, "You can't take him away from me! It's not fair."

Terry simply laughed.

I awoke with a start and shook my head, trying to erase the image, but Terry's laughter still boomed in my ears. I stood and laid my hand on Ron's arm. His ragged breathing told me he was awake.

"Darlin', have you been talking with Terry?"

He bent his toes.

"I just had a dream about him. He wants you to come be with him."

Yes.

"I told him you couldn't go, that I needed you here."

No response.

"Have you talked to your mother too?"

Yes.

Tears stung my eyes as I struggled to ask the next question. "Do you want to go and be with them?"

A moment passed with no reaction from Ron. Just as I let out a sigh of relief he moved his toes. *Yes.*

• • •

Sharon downloaded Pavarotti's arias to her iPad and set it on the foot of Ron's bed. I squeezed his swollen hand, which could no longer squeeze mine. I kissed his cheek.

"Darlin' I know you don't believe in an afterlife. But if you wake up and find yourself someplace else, please give me a sign so I know you're okay. Will you do that?"

Ron bent his toes. *Yes.*

One by one, Margot switched off the machines and removed the IVs from his body. A pulmonary nurse eased the ventilator hose from his throat. Ron's eyelids twitched. With difficulty he opened them and looked up at me, his blue eyes weak and watery.

"Go ahead, darlin'. Your family's waiting for you." I kissed his lips gently. "I will love you forever."

Ten minutes later his pulse stopped. I felt a light breeze ruffle my hair and thought I heard Ron's voice say, *Thank you, baby.*

PART TWO
DISCOVERING WHAT LIES BEYOND EARTH

"Death is nothing at all.
It does not count.
I have only slipped away into the next room.
Nothing has happened.

Everything remains exactly as it was.
I am I, and you are you,
and the old life that we lived so fondly together is
untouched, unchanged.
Whatever we were to each other, that we are still.

Call me by the old familiar name.
Speak of me in the easy way which you always used.
Put no difference into your tone.
Wear no forced air of solemnity or sorrow.

Laugh as we always laughed at the little jokes that we
enjoyed together.
Play, smile, think of me, pray for me.
Let my name be ever the household word that it always
was.
Let it be spoken without an effort, without the ghost of a
shadow upon it.

Life means all that it ever meant.
It is the same as it ever was.

There is absolute and unbroken continuity.
What is this death but a negligible accident?

Why should I be out of mind because I am out of
sight?
I am but waiting for you, for an interval,
somewhere very near,
just round the corner.

All is well.
Nothing is hurt; nothing is lost.
One brief moment and all will be as it was before.
How we shall laugh at the trouble of parting when we
meet again!"

-- Henry Scott Holland,
Canon of St. Paul's Cathedral, London,
and Oxford University professor (1847-1918)

CHAPTER 8

Shortly after I arrived home, neighbors began showing up with food, wine, and comforting hugs. My friend Anne, who'd driven me back from the hospital, had passed the word and I was grateful for the company.

How was I going to make it now, alone? Ron and I had maintained separate domiciles for most of our relationship. As a writer, I needed privacy and quiet in order to work. Ron's fiercely independent personality didn't lend itself well to cohabitation. However, we'd eaten dinner together nearly every evening, taken walks together in the afternoons, and talked on the phone twice a day. Now I would never again hear his voice or enjoy the great meals he cooked or snuggle against him at night. Life without him seemed too impossibly lonely to endure. The best I could hope for was that I would meet him again in a future lifetime.

After everyone left, I took a sleeping pill and drifted off--I'd slept so little the past four nights. I dreamed of seeing Ron in a place that reminded me of an ancient Roman bath, where numerous healers attended him. He seemed happy, vibrant, and younger than when I'd known him.

I thought I'd died, but here I am, better than ever, he told me in the dream.

I awoke feeling less afraid and more hopeful than when I'd gone to bed. Something about the dream felt genuine. I believed in the spirit's indestructability, an afterlife, and reincarnation, but my beliefs had never been put to such a grueling, up-close-and-personal test. Had I really witnessed Ron in his present state? Was he being cared for and healed in some heavenly realm after his lifetime on earth? Was he truly as happy as he appeared?

I brewed a pot of coffee and poured myself a cup, then set about the painful task of notifying Ron's many friends around the world of his passing. Everyone expressed the same shock and incomprehension. Like me, they'd expected this strong, healthy, vigorous man to live for many more years. Some regaled me with memories, stories that made me laugh and cry and gave me deeper insight into the man I loved. In the coming weeks, a few of them would send old photos I treasure.

Some, however, struck me as inconsiderate, cold, and downright rude. A family Ron had been close to since he first moved to Rockport, Massachusetts in the 1970s--people I knew too, and whom he'd considered a second family--ignored my phone calls and emails. A woman who'd once been my housemate, whom I'd thought of as a dear, longtime friend, didn't return my messages either. Were they at a loss for words? Did the intimacy of death frighten them? Alas, I'll never know, but in those early dark and desperate days I would have welcomed their condolences, which never came.

As dinnertime approached--a dinner I'd eat alone, staring at an empty place at the table--my phone rang. Cybele, the daughter of one of my close friends and a yoga instructor in Berkeley, California, who'd only met Ron a few times, wanted to tell me about something odd she'd experienced that afternoon while getting a massage.

"Thoughts of Ron filled my mind," she explained. "I strongly sensed his presence in the room with me. He seemed really happy and bathed in love."

I considered her choice of words, "bathed in love," and my dream about him in the Roman bath. We continued talking for a while, and I knew this was his way of fulfilling his promise to send a message from the other side to let me know he'd arrived in the afterlife.

Were Cybele's vision and my dream accurate? I hoped he was surrounded by peace and joy. Although he'd had plenty of fun during his time here on earth, Ron had rarely felt true joy and very little peace. I wanted that for him now.

• • •

Two days later, Ron's friend Louie telephoned from Switzerland. Only three weeks ago, Louie had visited Ron here in Texas. One morning during his stay, Louie told me in his German-accented English, Ron woke up late in the morning with a bad headache. He felt dizzy, tired, and had trouble getting out of bed. At the time Ron had chalked it up to sinus problems, popped a couple Excederin, and soldiered on.

"Now I think maybe he had a stroke," Louie said.

It seemed likely. Had Ron known? Why hadn't he mentioned the incident to me? If that was a preamble, if he'd realized something was wrong then, perhaps he could've gotten surgery to remedy the problem before it was too late.

I emailed Sharon and Elise and asked for their professional medical opinions. Within minutes, Elise emailed back. "With the aneurysm, the fistula, and the arteriovenus malformation, he might not have survived the surgery and may have had deficits even if he did. It is possible they may have excluded him as a surgical candidate. We just can't go there. But definitely that was a key sign that something was wrong. In the final analysis, his untimely death may have been the best way out."

Sadly, I had to agree with her. Of all the ways to exit this world, Ron's wasn't the worst. Certainly not as bad as what he'd talked about over the past year, with increasing regularity. "I'm about ready to eat a bullet," he said too way often. When his friend John gave him a shotgun, supposedly for self-defense, I started taking the threats more seriously. Now I tried to console myself that, finally, he'd found peace.

"Thanks for not shooting yourself," I said aloud to him. "And thanks for allowing me to be with you at the end."

From someplace just behind and slightly above my head I heard his voice answer, *You're welcome. I told you soon after I met you that you were my last woman.*

"Is that really you, Ron?"

Who else? You can't get rid of me that easily.

"I don't want to get rid of you ever. I want to be with you always."

And you will be. But you can't come over here where I am right now, so don't get any crazy ideas.

"Are you okay?" I wanted to think of him as the handsome, dynamic man I'd known before the stroke, not as someone lying helpless in a hospital bed.

Better than ever. Buck up now, baby, you've still got work to do where you are.

"What kind of work?"

Stick around and I'll show you.

CHAPTER 9

Next came the people who had money on their minds. Ron was always a generous man, and although he wouldn't have been considered rich by most standards, he'd earned a good salary as an air traffic controller, managed his money wisely, and lived debt-free.

Among those was his half-sister, Patty, in Wisconsin, whom I'd contacted after his passing. That I'd waited until after his death to call vexed her no end.

"If you'd let me know, I could've been there with him," she said in an accusatory tone.

"He didn't want a lot of fuss and people around him," I explained. "I asked him who he wanted there and I honored his wishes."

"How could you know what he wanted? He'd had a stroke, he couldn't talk."

"We could communicate up until the end. He was lucid the whole time."

I knew she didn't believe me and felt I was trying to shuttle her aside, although I'd asked Ron if he wanted her at his bedside and he'd replied *no*. He had little in common with his half-sister, their father's daughter from a first marriage, and didn't much like her. Nor did I. But Patty was the only family he had left, and to him that seemed reason enough for maintaining at least a perfunctory relationship.

Before long she contacted me again, this time via email. "By now you must know if Ron's trust/will has to go through probate. I will be watching for a copy of that and his death certificate in the mail. If it is too difficult or painful for you to send me a copy of his trust/will could you at least ask his attorney to do so or send me his name and address and I will ask him for it as I am sure with my being next of kin he wouldn't have a problem with that."

She hopes he made her his beneficiary, I thought. I shot back a terse response. "It will be probated in accordance with the laws of the state of Texas and Ron's written wishes. Anyone mentioned in it will be notified, as required by law. When that is finished, I'll send you a copy of the death certificate for your files. I understand your need for closure."

Shortly after Ron's passing, I'd also telephoned a Swedish friend of his named Karin, whom he'd known for decades. Like his half-sister, Karin questioned why I hadn't called her right away so she could have flown to Texas to say goodbye. I gave her the same answer I'd given Patty, adding that I didn't have her phone number with me when I was at the hospital, nor did I have international service on my cell phone. After promising to send me some early photos of Ron with her children, and asking me to mail her some of his ashes and T-shirts, we hung up.

A week later, Karin emailed me about Ron's will. "I am thinking about Ron and how he told me about his will. Since I do not live in the States I would also like to have his lawyer's name, so I can find out more of the procedure."

It came as no surprise. I emailed her back the same reply I'd sent to Patty, adding "Ron was very orderly, as you know, so things should go smoothly. I will meet with the attorney this afternoon and ask him if it's okay for you to call him so he can explain the process."

An old girlfriend in Hawaii showed her hand next. While Ron lay in St. Luke's Hospital's ICU, I'd stayed in touch by phone with Cheryl, who'd visited with us in Texas at Christmas a year ago. Only minutes before the pulmonary nurse removed his breathing tube, I'd dialed Cheryl's number and held my cell phone to Ron's ear so she could say her goodbyes.

"I was wondering if you checked on Ron's estate?" her email said. "Ron always said he was leaving me something."

How many more of these requests could I expect to receive? How many old lovers and friends had he promised to take care of? Ten? A hundred?

I emailed back, "It seems that over the years Ron told many people he'd put them in his will, and perhaps he did at one time. In 2008, he made his last will, which is with his attorney and will be probated according to Ron's written wishes and the laws of the state of Texas. I am the executrix of his estate. I know he cared very much about you, but I'm sorry to tell you that you're not mentioned in his will."

A few days later Cheryl emailed me again, this time on behalf of yet another former girlfriend, whom I'd notified after Ron passed. Judy and Ron had known each other for more than two decades and remained friends. According to Cheryl, Judy wanted some of his ashes. She also wanted the gifts she'd given Ron over the years returned to her.

"Really?" I said aloud as I stared at the email on the monitor. I stood up and began pacing back and forth across my office, the way I often did when I felt upset or angry. "Doesn't Judy understand the concept of gift-giving?"

After stomping about for a bit, I sat down at my computer and emailed back to Cheryl. "I have Judy's address and will send her some of Ron's ashes and send you some ashes separately. I would prefer that she contact me directly, instead of putting you in the middle—she's a big girl and can speak for herself."

Then I shot off an angry email to Elise. "You were right. What a bunch of greedy bitches have crawled out of the woodwork."

During all these conversations, I longed to confer with Ron and ask his advice. Everybody asked Ron for advice--his cool, pragmatic intelligence cut straight through the muddles that his friends often laid at his feet. Once upon a time, he'd gone to law school and would have excelled as a prosecutor. Later he applied that same analytical approach to people's personal problems. But when I tried to communicate with him about these women's demands, I sensed him laughing amiably. *You can handle it,* he said.

He has so much else to deal with now, I reminded myself. But as soon as I formed that thought he replied, *It's not about me. This is an opportunity for you to learn to take charge, without letting anyone intimidate you. Stay calm and detached. None of them has a leg to stand on. You're doing fine.*

• • •

Did I really hear Ron talking to me, I kept wondering? Or had I deluded myself, in my desperate need to believe his spirit still lived, that a connection continued to exist between us? That he was happy and still loved me?

When someone you love dies it feels like a meteorite has slammed into your world, blasting open a huge crater. The abyss stretches on and on, with no end in sight. You can't fill it in, the best you can do is find a way to walk around the hole in your life and keep on going.

Many of us are afraid we'll never see our loved ones again. Depending on our spiritual beliefs or lack of them, we may think the physical body's death marks the end. Lights out, done deal. Even if we hold a concept of an afterlife, we may worry that our loved ones might end up in a different place than we do. Or that we won't know where to find them in the vast otherworld when we, too, cross the rainbow bridge. What if they reincarnate before we do and become lost to us yet again?

According to all the books I've read on the subject, none of those fears is warranted. Nor are we ever truly separated from those who've moved to the other side. They're still with us and always will be.

We found each other before, we'll find each other again, I heard Ron say. *Don't worry, I'll be here to meet you when your time comes.*

One of my favorite poems is "Death Is Nothing at All"--a sermon, actually, that Canon Henry Scott Holland gave at St. Paul's Cathedral in London in 1910, while the body of King Edward VII was lying in state at Westminster. The author explains that the deceased has merely stepped into the next room and that the relationship you have with the person remains the same, even though you occupy different levels of reality.

This doesn't mean you won't suffer when a loved one passes from the physical world, even if you agree with Holland's view. You may grieve deeply and for a long time. Your life has been irrevocably changed. The larger the role the deceased played in it, the bigger the hole his or her passing rips in your everyday existence.

It's easier for me, Ron acknowledged. *I see you clearly, wherever you go, whatever you do. Of course, there's no such thing as time where I am now, so what you perceive of as weeks or months seems like only a moment to me.*

Then I heard him singing the old Beach Boys' song "Don't Worry Baby" and I could only hope that everything would, eventually, turn out all right.

• • •

Through the long, painful weeks that followed Ron's passing my friends held me together. They invited me to join them for lunch or dinner, brought me flowers and wine, took me for pedicures, facials, and massages. In the bleak times that swept me away like a riptide, I drank more than I should have in an attempt to dull the pain. I took sleeping pills to eek out a few hours of rest, hoping I wouldn't wake up--and when I did, I prayed it was all just a bad dream.

One morning my friend Anne, who'd been at the hospital with me when Ron passed, emailed to share "a remarkable experience" she'd had during a Reiki session. "The practitioner had my head resting in one of her hands with her other hand on my crown chakra. Suddenly, I thought of Ron. I was surprised (I hadn't been thinking about him), but I just went with it. Then I realized his energy was beside me . . . I strongly felt his presence. He spoke to me and said, *We all have a shot at Mastery.*"

I drew comfort from the knowledge that Ron was contacting people we both knew. It confirmed that he could, indeed, communicate from the other side--and did. In the following months, he regularly visited and talked to friends around the world. Each contact brought me hope and encouraged me to probe deeper into this new form of interaction that he and I were experiencing.

CHAPTER 10

On a friend's recommendation, I contacted a medium in New York. She refused to consult with me until later when I was, in her words, "less vulnerable." In the meantime, Ron stepped up his conversations with me. Through the desperately lonely days and endless nights, I sensed his presence near me, offering comfort and consolation.

Often, he sang to me. Initially I found this odd, because I'd never heard him sing while he was here on earth. He liked music well enough--especially the soul singers from the early sixties, disco, Celtic tunes, and most of all Pavarotti. He even liked rap--sometimes I teased him saying he was probably the only old white dude who did. Now, in response to my sadness and unspoken questions, he shared meaningful pieces from poignant songs with me. Dolly Parton's "I Will Always Love You." Randy Travis's "Forever and Ever Amen." Aaron Neville and Linda Ronstadt's "I Don't Know Much, But I Know I Love You."

When I asked him about this unexpected form of communication, he explained, *I was always a wannabe Irish tenor, but I couldn't carry a tune. Now that I'm no longer confined in my own body, I can use anyone else's voice to talk to you. When I was on earth I had trouble expressing my feelings. I never said a lot of things I wanted to say. Never managed to find the words--but they're all right there in the songs. So now I'll sing to you the things I wish I'd told you.*

But before I could ask him for more details, he was gone.

• • •

On earth, Ron had been a forceful and commanding individual. His job as an air traffic controller gave him the authority to issue orders pilots had to obey, if they wanted to continue flying. In his personal life, he demonstrated the same degree of self-confidence and authority--so much so that he sometimes came off as arrogant, judgmental, and brusque. He lived life on his own terms, for the most part, and anyone who didn't like it could hit the highway. His quick temper and harsh criticism often left me in tears.

As a spirit, however, he'd mellowed and become more philosophical. He didn't swear or yell or go off on extended tirades as he had when he was incarnate. His energy felt lighter and happier too. Now, I realized, he was communicating with me from a position of expanded consciousness. He was no longer the man I'd known, but a spirit with unlimited vision.

One morning while I sat in meditation, trying to quiet and open my mind to him, I heard him say in a playful tone, *You like me better now, don't you?*

"Well, you're easier to get along with."

I'm a kinder, gentler Ron. I laughed, and he continued. *I see things from a different perspective now. My core character hasn't changed, but the self-centeredness is gone. Here I'm not responsible for anyone else, just myself. That's a big relief. Plus we don't have all the annoyances and distractions you have on earth, and no egos to contend with.*

I remembered how much he'd abhorred stupidity. Answers came to him so quickly and clearly that he couldn't understand why other people didn't "get it." He never cut anyone any slack, least of all himself. As a result, his impatience often erupted into anger.

It's impossible to be narrow-minded over here. We see the ramifications of our thoughts immediately and don't go down roads that will turn out to be counterproductive. Yes, we have our disagreements, but because we're not attached to outcomes or the acquisition of personal power, like people on earth, we don't sweat the small stuff--we can focus on more important matters.

Suddenly the image of a mutual friend, an airline pilot who'd predeceased Ron, popped into my mind and waved to me, as if he were just passing through a room where we sat talking. The last time I'd seen Bob he'd been frail, withered, and suffering from terminal lung cancer. Now he appeared vibrant and cheerful, and about thirty years younger than when I knew him. Ron, too, looked to be about forty instead of the sixty-nine he'd been when he left his physical body.

Years later, two mediums would tell me that spirits often choose to present themselves as they were in the prime of their lives, or as they looked during the times when they felt most content. But they can assume any guise they wish. In many of his visits to me, Ron now resembled the youthful blond man in an old photo I kept in my office, a handsome, smiling thirty-eight-year-old who held the world in the palm of his hand, who had not yet suffered the crushing loss of his identical twin.

CHAPTER 11

Although I contemplated selling it, I decided to live in the house Ron bought after retiring from the Federal Aviation Administration. The house we'd picked out together and that now belonged to me.

He'd been the FAA's Operations Manager for New England during 9/11, and one of the first people to learn of the high-jacking of American Airlines' Flight 11. During the early days and weeks that followed he'd played a key role in handling the crisis. When air travel finally resumed to what would become the new normal, he decided he'd had enough. He was fed up with government bureaucracy and politics, tired of the seemingly endless Massachusetts winters, and opted for a quiet, secluded life in the heart of Texas.

Now, in the evenings, I sat on the back porch looking out over acres of live oaks, cactus, whitetail deer, and black buck antelope, and talked with Ron. We didn't actually "talk" in the usual manner, we communicated telepathically. I formed questions in my mind and received his immediate responses before I'd even finished my thoughts. Sometimes I "heard" his words, but more often an awareness flashed in my mind, like a spark of light, and I had to translate his side of the conversation into cohesive sentences. Often I felt him stroking my hair as he'd affectionately done when he was human. I smelled his scent, too, like cinnamon and cloves.

Birth, death, rebirth--it's like a revolving door, he said. *You move from one space into another, hang out there for a while, and then when you're ready you go through the door again and emerge someplace else. No big deal.*

"Are you here?" I asked.

He began singing the Beatles' song "Here, There, and Everywhere." *There's really no "here" or "there," and no past or future either. Those are illusions.*

"So where are you now? Where did you go when you left your physical body?"

Home. This is where we come from and return to, again and again. Except it's not a place, exactly. And it's not separate from where you are. Think of it as a reality that exists at a different vibratory level than earth's, which is why you can't see it. Think about radio stations that operate simultaneously, but you can't hear them all at the same time because they're playing at different frequencies.

"Is your brother there?"

Yes, and so is everyone else who's ever lived on earth. When I went to Catholic school the nuns told us only baptized Christians got into the kingdom of heaven, but that's not true. St. Peter doesn't stand at the pearly gate and go through a checklist to decide if you're worthy to come inside. This isn't some sort of elite fraternity that excludes people because they didn't get dunked or sprinkled properly, or didn't accept this or that guy as their savior.

I turned the idea over in my mind: Everybody gets in. How many wars have been fought over the ages, based on the belief that certain people with certain ideologies were superior to others and thus favored by God? I thought about how much fear and suffering people endure, believing their so-called sins might bar them from "heaven." What if we understood we are all part of a greater whole? What if we realized our innate goodness? And that even if we screw up royally in one particular earth life, we won't be condemned to eternal damnation? Instead, we'll be granted another chance to set things right.

Other kinds of spirits live here too, Ron continued. *Some of them have never been physical.*

That made me think about two beautiful childlike beings I often sensed near me, whose lighthearted and playful presence always brought me a glimmer of joy. They accompanied me wherever I drove, bouncing about in the backseat like fun-loving kids. I called them Megan and Moriah.

Ron read my mind. *They've never been to earth. That's probably why they're so happy. Earth's a hard place for souls to endure. None of us goes to earth for the purpose of being happy, although that can and does happen. Even the harshest lives contain moments of happiness.*

"Then why do souls incarnate here?"

Sometimes we want to be with other souls we love who've returned to earth. Maybe we see a situation in which we believe we can be of use, or an opportunity that we feel could help us grow, or a chance to exercise our creativity. Sometimes we think we've gained enough knowledge between lives that we can do a better job next time around. But there's a catch. While we're here, at home, we understand the truth. When we take physical forms again, we're subject to the illusions that exist on earth and we forget what we knew before going back. Whatever the reason, it's always the soul's choice to put on a human body again.

"You mean we're not required to come to earth?"

No, we're not required to do anything. We decide, with the help of guides and teachers and other souls, if we want to incarnate. If we feel we can learn something useful from the experience of being human, we make the arrangements--who we'll be, when, where, and so on.

I was familiar with the earth-as-a-school theory and the concept of reincarnation. However, I'd always believed we all had to spend time on Planet Earth, gradually working our way up the spiritual ladder, until we finally learned what we needed to know and graduated to an exalted position, at which point we never had to assume physical form again. I thought about Jesus and the Buddha and other enlightened teachers, as well as discarnate entities I'd read about, such as Seth and Emmanuel.

Yes, some do reach that pinnacle, Ron told me. *Your guide Grace, for instance, is pretty advanced. She doesn't have to return to earth anymore. Still, there are many others above her.*

For as long as I could remember, I'd been aware of a loving and serene being guiding and protecting me. I knew her as Grace, a sort of guardian angel whom I imagined was garbed in pure white light. To me, she epitomized peace and goodness.

Grace has been with you forever, in other lifetimes as well as this one. Now I'm guiding you too, Ron said. *I'm what you might call your immediate contact. Your go-to guy. I'm never more than a thought away and you can call on me whenever you want. You're my responsibility now--you bear watching, you know.*

I laughed at his last words, which I'd heard often enough during our time together on earth. He always thought I needed constant direction and protection, that I'd surely make a mess of things if left to my own devices, even though I'd somehow managed to get along for fifty years before meeting him.

Oh, and by the way, your cat's here too. Megan and Moriah are taking care of her.

"Domino?"

My beloved feline friend of nearly nineteen years suffered a fatal aneurism six months prior to Ron's passing. We'd buried her body in the backyard, under a limestone boulder she liked to sit on and sun herself. As I looked at the boulder with my physical eyes, a picture arose in my mind's eye: my beautiful black-and-white cat sitting between the two youthful spirits. Ron reached over, lifted her paw, and waved it at me in a way that reminded me of a Chinese *maneki-neko.*

"You mean animals live where you are now too?"

All kinds of animals. Not only cats and dogs, but also long-extinct creatures and some that never lived on earth--or haven't yet.

Being an animal lover, I couldn't imagine I would be happy in an afterlife that didn't include animals, although I'd wondered sometimes if they had their own "heaven." In her book *The Light Between Us,* medium Laura Lynne Jackson wrote about seeing many animals on the other side in a psychic reading she did for two people who had devoted their lives to rescuing creatures in need. I certainly believed animals had souls, even though I realized many people didn't agree with me. Plus animals' patience, devotion, and willingness to sacrifice themselves so we can live made them superior to people, in my opinion. Perhaps animals have shorter lifespans than humans because they already understand the purpose of existence is to love--they don't need to learn that lesson, they only want to teach it to us.

As I contemplated what Ron had said, I noticed an armadillo scuttling through the grass. Even though it dug holes in my yard, I liked watching this odd-looking animal with its armored body. "Tell me more about the creatures that haven't lived on earth yet."

Animals--and humans too--begin their development over here, before they go to earth. Spirits experiment with different designs to see which ones might be best suited to take on physical forms. Some work out for a period of time, like the dinosaurs, but then leave earth for various reasons. Armadillos, you know, have been around longer than practically any other mammals--a very effective design. As the planet evolves, so do the species that live on it. The Ice Age destroyed some species, global warming is killing off others. But new ones will develop. For example, we have prototypes here of creatures that will chow down on plastic and Styrofoam.

"Sounds like a good idea, considering the whole world's becoming a big garbage dump."

Sometimes we take pieces of one species and graft them onto another to create a composite that's more resilient or adaptable to changing conditions.

Pictures of the half-animal, half-human deities in Egyptian mythology arose in my mind. Before I could ask about them, Ron answered.

They actually existed, but not in dense bodies like humans. So do mermaids and other mythical creatures. They function at a different resonance than humans, which is why people can't see them most of the time. Once in a while the signals get crossed and somebody spots them, but they're not physical the way you are--

that's why nobody's found any mermaid bones or unicorn horns.

"How's all that square with Darwin's theory of evolution?"

Old Charlie was a material guy and that limited his ability to see and interpret the big picture. He could only explain the physical side of things. He didn't understand that everything on earth originates on the plane of imagination. Let me give you an analogy: Before a house can get built an architect has to imagine it. He'll do drawings, maybe make a model to be sure the pieces fit together right. The physical structure is the last step in the process.

I pondered the idea while the armadillo finished his tour of my backyard and wiggled through a hole in the fence. A family of deer trotted up the hill as they did every evening around this time, hoping for a handout. Such a vast assortment of entities shared the planet with me, I mused with awe and wonder. It must be fun to be part of the team that designs them.

Ron chuckled, reading my thoughts. *Go feed the deer some tortillas. We'll talk more later.*

CHAPTER 12

Ron's comments had sparked my curiosity. Even as a young child, I'd wondered where I came from, why I was here, where I'd go when I died, and so on. I'd never felt comfortable on earth and had a hard time reconciling my physical self with the "inner me" who seemed like a stranger in a strange land. It was as if I were watching the world through someone else's eyes.

This disconnect and my desire for understanding led me to explore many metaphysical areas over the years: ESP, astrology, tarot, as well as mythology and holistic healing. My passion for knowledge evolved into a publishing career, and I've written many books about subjects that have intrigued and informed me. Now another door had opened and I felt compelled to walk through it.

I wanted to know more about the place Ron called "home." What was it like to be disembodied? How did souls in his world interact? What did they do with their time? Questions raced through my mind, and each one spawned another. During my morning meditation, I asked him to tell me more about home.

I'll do more than tell you, I'll take you there, he replied.

Did he mean I was going to die? My eyes snapped open, my body stiffened in anticipation. Apparently, Ron intuited my apprehension because he gently stroked my hair and spoke softly to me, the way one might calm a frightened animal. *Remember the cosmic consciousness experience you had when you were thirty-two?*

The term "cosmic consciousness" as described by the Canadian psychiatrist Richard Bucke refers to a heightened awareness in which human beings perceive the cosmos as alive and eternal, "that the universe is God and that God is the universe, and that no evil ever did or ever will enter into it." In this mystical state, one understands that all beings are part of a unified whole, held together by the infinite and indestructible force of love.

Like many people who've described experiencing cosmic consciousness, I slipped into this rarified state unintentionally, without even knowing it existed. One minute I was sitting on my bed, lamenting my lack of direction and purpose and my general dissatisfaction with pretty much every part of my life at the time. In the next, my bedroom and everything in it, as well as my body, suddenly dissolved in a sea of glowing pink light.

I felt surrounded and suffused by an extraordinary, ineffable presence of unconditional love. The physical world, my sense of self, and time disappeared. I had no awareness of anything except the all-encompassing love and the radiant light in which I was immersed.

How much time elapsed I'll never know. A minute? Ten? An hour or more? At some point, I slid back into my ordinary consciousness, but the memory of that transcendent experience remains to this day. I consider it one of the most exquisite and beautiful moments of my entire life. *Silly You can have it daiey*

Although I'd never mentioned this to Ron, he not only knew about it, but could explain it to me. *You came home for a brief visit then. That's what it's like where I am. If you want to, you can come back again now, but you can't stay--you still have work to do on earth. Just relax and I'll guide you.*

Slowly I eased into a deep, trancelike state. I soon became aware of a disconnect between my mind and body, as if one part of me was struggling to free itself from the other. My physical body felt heavy and dense. An inexplicable weight pressed down on my shoulders while an effervescent energy pushed upward, like an underground stream longing to burst through to the surface. After a few moments of discomfort, I felt a sensation of weightlessness as if I were riding in a high-speed elevator to the top of a skyscraper. Then the inner part of me separated from the physical part and soared into a world beyond.

Weightless, I drifted through a soft, pale pink cloud that enveloped me completely. A faint humming filled my ears. I could no longer distinguish my body; it seemed to have melted into the cloud. Then the cloud began to glow with a beautiful pink-and-gold light and I felt bathed in love.

Gradually, the cloud parted. Ron stood beside me. Although he looked pretty much as he had on earth, he wasn't solid--he was made entirely of radiant, golden light.

I gazed out at the scenario that stretched before me endlessly, and saw orbs of light reaching far into the distance--mostly white ones, but also yellow and gold, plus a few green, blue, and purple. The orbs pulsed and bobbed, all clustered so close to one another that they looked like soap bubbles floating in a bathtub. Somehow I knew they were sentient. Above everything hung the wondrous pink glow, like a delicate net of shimmering silk holding the orbs together.

"What are they?" I whispered.

Souls. This is our home, where we come between lifetimes on earth or in other places.

"Why are they different colors?" Were souls divided into races in the otherworld, the way human beings were on earth, I wondered.

The colors reflect their levels of knowledge and awareness, sort of like cosmic karate belts. Don't think in terms of earthly accomplishment, though. Here "progress" comes as a result of awakening more and more. The white ones are the most immature, like babies learning to crawl. You could liken the yellow ones to teenagers, and the gold ones to mature adults. They assist people on earth. The green ones care for the planet and nature. The blue ones are more advanced souls--they're teachers and senior guides. The purple ones are the wisest and most advanced masters.

"You're a gold soul," I said, referring to the glow that emanated from him. "Is that why you take care of me?"

You and other people, yes. DISAGREE ME HAS A WAY TO GO

I thought about the countless people he'd guided ANYWAY safely through the skies during his thirty-seven years as an air traffic controller.

"Do the different souls interact with each other?" I asked.

Well, we're all connected, we're all part of the whole. But not everyone hangs out with everyone else. We form groups according to our interests and similarities, as well as what we're working on at any particular time--just like people on earth do. We don't all get along either, although we manage to work things out better than humans do because we can't hide our thoughts and feelings from each other. We understand instantly how to resolve our differences.

"What's that pink light glowing around everything?" I remembered how it had embraced me as I entered this transcendent world.

That's the resonance of love. It serves as a buffer between harsh energies, softening and smoothing them so discord dissipates as soon as it arises. Among other things, we learn to manage conflicts here. If only we

IN like SUICIDAL ANGRY DISCONTENT HOW is this DEATH complete?

could remember that when we return to earth, life there would be so much more pleasant.

I tried to hold on to the immense sensation of love and harmony that shimmered all around me, hoping I might, indeed, remember it when I returned to my ordinary life. I wanted to commit it to memory, like a perfect sunset seen on an idyllic vacation. Even if I only managed to bring back a spark of the peace I felt in this wondrous place, it could help me cope with the stress and confusion that dominated my days.

Wishing I could tuck a packet of pink light in my pocket as a keepsake, I asked Ron, "Do souls group together according to color?"

Pretty much. Most of those in my group are gold, a few yellow and blue ones. We guide humans in their progress on earth. I don't have anything to do with the white souls--not due to prejudice, I just don't have any reason to associate with them. They don't know enough yet to help themselves, let alone anyone else. Higher forces exist beyond the blue and purple souls, but I don't interact with them directly. I don't know how many there are or even what they are, only that they exist. Ultimately, though, we're all linked by light--to each other as well as to beings on earth and elsewhere.

Fascinated, I watched the surging sea of colored, glowing orbs. To me, they looked like an amorphous, undulating mass. How did they relate to each other? How did they communicate? What did they do here? Questions tripped over each other in my mind.

"How many souls are in your group?"

Overall, about a hundred, but only twenty-one make up my inner circle.

"What's an 'inner circle'?"

An intimate group of souls to whom I'm connected forever--here, on earth, and elsewhere in the universe. What some people might call soul mates. The bonds between us are eternal. We reincarnate together again and again to learn from each other, but we also just want to be together.

"Am I part of your inner circle?" I asked, hoping I ranked among his select few.

Yes. We'll be together always, though I won't always be your lover. In another lifetime I might be your father or sister or friend. Some circles overlap, too, like the rings in the Olympics logo. As he spoke, a picture of the five interlocking rings flashed in my mind. *Some beings in my inner circle might also be in yours, but not everyone is. My brother Terry, for instance, isn't part of your group and your friend Lyndsey isn't in mine.*

He embraced me then, our two light-bodies joining in a more loving and intimate contact than I'd ever experienced in physical form, and I felt suffused with joy.

This is how we hold each other when we're no longer embodied, he told me.

When we're incarnate, our physical bodies keep us separate from one another--the closest we can get is during sex. Without the limitations of form, however, our energy fields can merge and we experience perfect union. We immerse ourselves in the infinite love that is the source of everything, the ultimate creative force of the universe.

I'm going to take you back now. But soon I'll show you a lot more, beyond your wildest dreams.

Slowly, I became aware of my physical body again, then the chair in my bedroom where I sat. A pleasant tingling sensation resonated through me as I settled back into my ordinary human form. After a while, I opened my eyes. Although it was midday, the room seemed dark in comparison to the brilliant light I'd witnessed in Ron's world.

I must have fallen asleep, I thought. Such a lovely dream.

It's no dream, I heard him say.

"You mean I was really there, with you?"

Yes, and you can come back here anytime you want. A piece of you remains here all the time. You only take part of your soul-energy with you when you go to earth, the rest stays at home.

I tried to imagine a piece of me remaining on the other side while the rest of me hung out here on earth. How much energy had I left behind, comfortable and secure at home? What was that part doing while I muddled through my everyday life in a physical body? Before I could explore those thoughts, however, Ron told me something even more astonishing.

When a soul decides to go back to earth, some of us--especially those in the soul's inner circle--gather around and help to prepare it for re-embodiment. We're like trainers and coaches prepping an athlete for a big game. He showed me a picture of him rolling golden light in his hands, molding it into a ball. *We even give the reincarnating soul pieces of our own energy to take along on the journey, sort of like good luck charms. You have a little bit of my energy in you.*

Feeling overwhelmed, I said, "I need time to digest all this."

Write it down so you don't forget.

• • •

During the long, cold New England winter of 2001, I'd discovered quite by accident that our souls radiate with different colors. While I was meditating beside the gas-burning stove Ron had installed in my drafty, antique house, I saw people I knew as glowing orbs of colored light instead of the flesh-and-blood humans I believed them to be. I was a sunny yellow sphere, Ron a radiant gold one. My former husband appeared as an emerald green ball of light, my friend Lyndsey a pale blue one with a funny pseudopodium that propelled her about at high speed.

The images had nothing to do with auras--I'd seen and worked with auras before and there was no similarity. Auras show the energies emanating from someone's physical and emotional bodies, and shift in connection with the person's feelings, health, and other conditions. The colors I saw reflected my friends' levels of soul development, although I didn't know that at the time. I merely noted it as an interesting idea. Because I'm an artist, I decide to paint what I'd observed. "Soul portraits" you might call them.

Twelve years later, after Ron had gone home, I started reading everything I could about the afterlife, desperately trying to understand my life as it was now. I immediately felt drawn to Dr. Michael Newton's books and still consider them some of the best ones I've found on the subject of life between lives.

Newton, a hypnotherapist in California, regressed thousands of clients and wrote about their explorations into past lives as well as to the worlds they inhabited between earthly existences. In his first book, *Journey of Souls,* he discussed things Ron had told me about, including souls' inner circles. Newton defined these as clusters of between three and twenty-five souls and wrote, "Members of the same cluster group are closely united for all eternity." Just how Ron described them!

Newton also outlined a cosmic classification of souls by color. According to him, white souls are beginners, yellow souls intermediate beings, gold ones upper-level intermediates, blue souls advanced beings. The rare purple ones are highly advanced souls.

Again, Newton's assessments validated what Ron had told me and what I'd witnessed myself, although in my earliest explorations I hadn't connected colors with levels of soul development. At the time I observed them, I had no idea what I was seeing and attached no significance to my observations. Furthermore, I'd also seen a few green and black souls in my sojourns, but Newton didn't mention these in his book.

Six years later, in his follow-up book *Destiny of Souls,* Newton plunged deeper into the afterlife. He revealed more of what he'd discovered by regressing patients to their past personalities and the worlds between lives. Again, his research confirmed what I'd experienced--and in this book, I was pleased to find, he spoke of encountering green and black souls too.

● ● ●

Under hypnosis, Dr. Newton's regressed patients also delighted in the wonders of the place they, like Ron, called home.

"Oh wonderful, I'm home in this beautiful place again," the newly deceased exclaimed.

"It's such a quiet place . . . I feel . . . love . . . companionship . . . empathy."

Some described hearing exquisite music, others said "this space is infinite . . . so majestic . . . and peaceful."

According to Newton, "my subjects are full of exclamations about rediscovered marvels of the spirit world. Usually, this feeling is combined with euphoria that all their worldly cares have been left behind . . . Above all else, the spirit world represents a place of supreme quiescence."

A few years later I watched a video module in Dr. Piero Calvi-Parisetti's course *Love Knows No Death,* in which a number of people who'd undergone near-death experiences shared their memories of home. Like Newton's patients, they described the profound joy and unconditional love that enveloped them in this mystical realm. Their descriptions echoed my own experience of cosmic consciousness and the glorious pink-lit environment I'd witnessed when I visited Ron's home.

"It was total bliss, total love, total acceptance," one person said. "I felt like that's where I belonged."

"I'm filled with a love and a peace that I cannot explain," another said.

"Everything's fine and always will be and always has been," another explained.

Like Ron, these people were supremely happy in the world beyond. None of them wanted to return to earth and its hardships.

Despite my own grief and loneliness, I was glad for Ron. Glad he'd finally found the peace and joy that had eluded him during his most recent incarnation, and glad he'd reunited with loved ones he thought he'd lost forever.

I only wished I could be there with him.

CHAPTER 13

If the afterlife is as glorious as those who've been there insist, why are we afraid of death? Maybe we don't really believe all the glowing accounts we've read, or we dread the fatal event that will jar us loose from our physical forms and into the next dimension.

Although the illness or injury that causes physical death may be painful, it seems "death" itself is not. In *Love Knows No Death*, a woman who had undergone a near-death experience explained, "All the pain went away and I was in an ethereal body that was perfect." Dr. Raymond A. Moody, Jr., in his book *Life After Life*, quotes a man who described his death in Vietnam as "A great attitude of relief. There was no pain and I've never felt so relaxed. I was at ease and it was all good."

According to *Emmanuel's Book III* of channeled communications from an advanced discarnate being and compiled by Pat Rodegast and Judith Stanton, "Death is not traumatic to the dying. One moment you are alive and then you are not, and there is little difference except you are free . . . death itself is always most pleasant to those who have died."

As I mentally asked Ron about this, I heard the old song "Everybody Wants to Go to Heaven, but Nobody Wants to Die" playing in my mind.

Mostly we're afraid of the unknown--and death is the ultimate unknown for human beings, he replied. *Then there's the control factor. People like me, who tried to control everything in our earth lives, don't like surprises. Not knowing the rules or what to expect and not having any power to direct what's happening to us is terrifying. Plus we're scared of being judged and punished--remember, many of us have been raised with ideas of hellfire and damnation. We fear we're going to have to face a heavenly court, and they'll probably find us guilty and condemn us for our sins.*

I knew he was right. Most people have been taught fear instead of love. Many believe we're born in sin--before we even take our first breaths we're doomed. Our shortcomings and mistakes are pointed out *ad infinitum,* but our inherent beauty gets little recognition or support.

So, what actually happens when we die? Although not everyone undergoes exactly the same things and some folks only witness some of the stages researchers identify with the near-death experience, quite a large number of those who return from an NDE share similar stories. Many of them speak of floating above their lifeless bodies, watching loved ones crying or medical personnel attempting life-saving procedures. Some of these people even describe in great detail what occurred while they were out of their bodies. During this initial phase of separation, the soul may not realize the body that once housed it has died. It may wonder what all the fuss is about or try to get the attention of people nearby.

Next, the soul travels through a dark tunnel toward a brilliant white light at the end. After emerging from the tunnel and into that light, the soul is met by relatives, friends, spirit guides, and/or holy figures who welcome it back home. This meeting is almost always described as being incredibly joyful and the soul feels wrapped in unconditional love. It may also experience the presence of an omnipotent and omniscient divine being.

Some people observe scenes from their earth lives at this point. In *Life After Life*, Dr. Raymond Moody recollects one man's account: "I could remember everything; everything was so vivid . . . The best thing I can think of to compare it to is a series of pictures, like slides." Others say they were privy to an infinite knowledge of the cosmos. A man who spoke on a video for *Love Knows No Death* described it this way: "I was part of the light, and once I was in the light I knew everything that the light knew. I knew all about the universe."

In some cases, newly arrived souls are ushered into an orientation area where spirits help them get used to being home again. Even though they're returning to the place from which they originated, for some the experience can be confusing at first. People who had no conception of an afterlife while they were on earth and those who feared death, as well as those who left their bodies suddenly and without warning--due to an accident, heart attack, or injury, for example--may need time to adjust to this transition.

These occurrences are frequently reported by those who have undergone near-death experiences, as well as by those who've been regressed to prior lifetimes and deaths. However, not everyone witnesses the same events, in the same order.

In some cases, NDErs describe going to places that resemble their preconceived notions of paradise. Some may linger for a while in a sort of vague "no man's land" feeling lost and confused. And some people, after being revived, don't remember anything at all.

More than a century ago, a Massachusetts doctor named Duncan MacDougall attempted to provide scientific evidence of the soul's departure from the physical body at the exact moment of death. In an experiment he conducted on April 10, 1901, Dr. MacDougall, accompanied by four other physicians, weighed a patient with tuberculosis right before his death and immediately after the man died. Oddly, the newly dead body weighed three-quarters of an ounce (twenty-one grams) less than it had only moments before. This led the doctors to surmise that the soul had substance that could be measured. In subsequent years, MacDougall performed the same experiment on several other patients with similar results, which were published in the *New York Times* in 1907. However, his research has been criticized due to the small number of patients and irregularities in his procedures.

Belief in an afterlife isn't new, of course--many early cultures embraced it. Mythology and religious texts offer myriad descriptions of the process of dying, death, and the hereafter. According to Norse myths, fallen warriors went on to live into a majestic palace known as Valhalla where the god Odin presided. The ancient Egyptians held numerous and elaborate rituals, including embalming, designed to guide the soul in its passage from this world to the next. Once it reached the other side, a deity named Ma'at weighed the soul against the feather of truth to determine if it was light enough to enter the spirit realm.

Both Hindus and Buddhists assert that the soul is eternal. *The Tibetan Book of the Dead* describes the death experience from a Buddhist perspective and discusses six realms of existence prior to and following physical death. It explains the soul's progress from a state of luminosity shortly before death, during which a person gives up struggling to the realm of the gods, the final stage of self-realization, comfort, and peace. Both Hindus and Buddhists believe that souls go through numerous earthly incarnations, until eventually they achieve perfection and reunite with the Source.

Many centuries ago, the Bible contained accounts of reincarnation, but these were largely excised at the Council of Nicaea in 325 C.E. Christians continue to uphold a concept of heaven, though, where "good" souls reside after the body dies.

In the late 1800s and early 1900s, Spiritualists in England and the U.S. explored the world beyond via mediumship, séances, and other practices, in hopes of contacting the spirits of the dead--even England's Queen Victoria and Prince Albert attended séances. Anyone who chooses to delve into the subject further will find a wealth of information available.

It seems we humans have pondered for millennia the transition from earth to a spiritual world, and we probably will continue doing so into the foreseeable future. Life's greatest mystery has yet to be solved.

CHAPTER 14

As I rummaged around in the freezer, searching for leftovers to warm up for dinner, I spotted a package of spaghetti sauce Ron had made eleven days before his stroke. In neat, precise letters he'd labeled the package and dated it. I'd read that everyone's handwriting is different, like fingerprints, and you can tell all sorts of things about someone from his handwriting. I stared at Ron's unique combination of upper and lowercase letters, and ran my finger over them lovingly. Fighting back tears, I grabbed a container of chili instead and shut the freezer door.

Dinnertime used to be my favorite part of the day. Now it was the hardest. Ron liked to cook and most evenings he prepared the meals we enjoyed together. In winter we dined by candlelight or in front of the fireplace; in spring and summer fresh flowers graced the table. While I stood at the stove warming the chili, I heard Ron's voice. If he were still here in the flesh he would have been issuing instructions, a chef directing his staff.

Now he calmly explained the process of dying.

We leave earth in stages, he told me. *We start gradually detaching from the physical world and begin the journey back home long before our bodies actually die--even if we seem to go quickly, like I did. The decision was made quite a while ago. Most people aren't aware of doing it, though.*

Years ago, Ron told me he wanted to die of a stroke before he turned seventy. At the time, I hadn't given it much credence, shelving the idea at the back of an out-of-the-way bookcase in my mind. Seventy wasn't old, especially for someone as strong and healthy as Ron. By the time he celebrated his sixty-ninth birthday in Hawaii with a group of friends, six months before he passed, I'd forgotten all about his pronouncement.

But that's exactly what happened. Now I wondered, had he known in advance he'd leave earth this way? Had he consciously orchestrated his final exit?

While the chili heated, I scissored fresh spinach into a bowl and cut up tomatoes, carrots, and an avocado for a salad.

"Your friend Louie said you had a stroke when he visited here in March. Is that true?"

Yes. But I began planning my escape even before that. I think I started leaving after Terry died. Each person decides his own time, place, and method. There's no such thing as an "untimely death." No one dies one moment earlier or later than he chooses. Even a life that lasts only a day can be immensely important.

"If that's the case, why would anyone choose to get blown apart in war or buried alive in an avalanche?" I thought about his brother's battle with brain cancer and he read my mind as he often did.

100

For all sorts of reasons. Some souls decide to suffer through long, drawn-out illnesses to give doctors a chance to study them and learn ways to help people in the future.

"What about people in nursing homes? Why do they pick such a sad, demeaning end?"

Maybe they want to give their caretakers a chance to show compassion, or maybe they need to learn how to accept kindness from other people. I learned a lot when I was in the hospital at the end, totally dependent on you and the medical staff. That was a new thing for me--all my life I'd always been the one in charge.

At the time, I'd felt terrible seeing him completely helpless and immobile in that hospital bed, knowing how humiliated he must have been, stripped of his dignity, strength, and freedom. I'd even felt guilty for dragging out his suffering instead of letting him go home sooner. Now, though, I understood we'd made that agreement together, to gain experiences we both needed.

Some choose to die for a cause, he continued.

"That seems awfully noble."

They don't see it that way.

For centuries soldiers have fought and given their lives to protect their lands, their people, and their ways of life. I thought about the IRA prisoners during The Troubles in Ireland in the 1980s, who protested with hunger strikes and died. I could even imagine that Martin Luther King and Mahatma Gandhi may have opted for assassination in order to focus attention on their causes. But why did millions of Jews perish at the hands of the Nazis, or countless innocent women burn as witches during the Inquisition's reign of terror? And what about the children gunned down at Sandy Hook Elementary School? I shook my head, struggling to get my mind around what was impossible to comprehend, and failed.

I'll explain more later, when I tell you about my life review, Ron promised. *You better stir that chili or it's going to burn.*

I turned off the stove and scooped chili into a bowl, then sprinkled grated cheddar on top and uncapped a bottle of India pale ale. "Join me for dinner?"

Sure, but I'd have preferred spaghetti.

• • •

The idea of life review intrigued me, and a few days later I asked Ron to elaborate. "How's your 'life review' going?"

It's going. It takes a while to process through sixty-nine earth years.

"I thought your whole life flashed before your eyes the instant you died."

Nope, a common misconception. People who have near-death experiences describe it that way, but they're usually only "dead" for a short period of time. It's not the real deal, they're just testing the waters.

"But they're clinically dead, aren't they?" I asked.

According to technical medical definitions and instruments that measure the body's vitals, yes. But that's not the whole story.

Apparently, Ron agreed with author Mary Roach, who put it succinctly in her book *Spook*: "Clinically dead is not *dead* dead."

While we're in human form, an energetic cord connects the soul and body--you've heard it called a silver cord or an aka cord. When someone has an NDE, that cord remains attached. It's only severed when a soul finally calls it quits and decides to go home. A person who undergoes an NDE may see glimpses of the life he's led on earth, but he doesn't ever get to the stage of what we call life review. Life review usually follows a period of reorientation, adjustment, healing, R&R--whatever the soul needs or chooses as it eases back into life out of the physical body. It's not a first step in homecoming.

An image popped into my mind of a group of beings, seated in a circle around a glowing orb about the size of a beach ball. The orb reminded me of a holograph, reflecting moving pictures. The beings gathered around it glowed too. Shaped vaguely like humans sitting in lotus position, they resembled statues of the Buddha-- except they were made entirely of light that rippled like the aurora borealis and they appeared to float. Among them I recognized Ron's golden light and realized he was showing me a glimpse of his experience.

These are my teachers and spirit guides, he explained. *We sit together and examine everything I did during my life on earth.*

"Everything?"

He laughed. *Well, not every email I sent or every meal I ate. But every significant action I took, every interaction with someone else, every meaningful thought or feeling I had. Together we consider all of them and their ramifications. My guides show me scenes from my life in retrospect, like a 3-D movie, but they don't judge me or tell me what I should do. There's no ego involved. Ego disappears when you leave the body, so I can be objective as I assess my past.*

That's what the ball with the pictures did, I realized. It projected a sort of cosmic home movie so he could witness his life as Ron.

I don't have to go through it chronologically. I can choose what I want to review from any moment in my life--rewind, fast-forward, pause. And I can do it at my own pace, just so long as I eventually complete the whole thing. Seeing how I affected other people is the hardest part. I not only watch what happened, I feel it all again. What's more, I feel it from the perspectives of everyone else who was involved too.

He paused for a moment, as if considering how to express what he wanted to say. *I realized I'd hurt people. A lot of people. Women mostly. Not intentionally, but my ego and my own desires prevailed. I wasn't always kind to the women who cared about me.*

104

And fear always stood in the way of love. Fear interfered, he punned. *I feared commitment, on every level.*

"But so many people loved and admired you. You should hear all the wonderful things they say about you."

Be that as it may, he continued. *I never meant to hurt you, Skye. I wanted us to spend a lot more time together. We'd talked about doing so many things when we had more time. But we never did. My fault.*

He paused again, and I sensed him turning over memories, viewing his life on earth in the light of his new understanding. *Until I came home and started doing my life review, I never thought much about what I did on earth, except in a very narrow, self-serving way. It's hard for human beings to get outside themselves and see things from another person's perspective. One thing I've learned here that I never considered before: Kindness is important. It's rarely modeled for us on earth and we often connect it with weakness. Now I know I could've handled things better. I have to decide how to make restitution to the people I harmed.*

I contemplated the Hindu concept of karma and the Old Testament idea of an eye for an eye. "How do you go about making restitution?"

My guides don't insist on recompense or punishments in the sense humans do. Sometimes all that's necessary is to witness and acknowledge what happened, with honesty and humility, without making excuses or trying to dodge the truth. It depends on how the other person responds too. Sometimes I can apologize to the person I harmed and he or she accepts my apology, then we can move on from there. And sometimes an action will be required in a future existence to re-establish balance. Karma isn't about punishment or payback, it's about achieving balance.

He paused for a bit. I waited to see if he'd continue, remembering how annoyed he got when I interrupted him.

I never wanted to get old. And I was so awfully tired of being on earth. When I had the stroke, I saw my out and I took it. Please know that I didn't leave to get away from you--you were the best thing in my life. I heard him singing a line from the old Manhattans' hit "You Are My Shining Star." *I wanted to get away from everything else, though. I was so done with all that.*

"But you had such a good life."

I had everything we're supposed to want. You know, the American Dream.

"So what went wrong?"

My life was both happy and sad. You and I had problems, but we also had a lot of happiness together. I had plenty of good times throughout my life too. But underneath it all lay a deep sadness I couldn't erase. After my brother died, I realized that no matter what I did, how hard I tried, what I loved most could be destroyed in a heartbeat and I was powerless to prevent it. I never managed to release the pain inside me.

Tears slid down my cheeks. "I'm so sorry, Ron. I wish we'd talked about these things while you were here, really talked. Our early lives scarred us so much."

I died from grief and loneliness. Yes, I know, the medical report called it a "stroke" but behind every physical condition lies an emotional one. Doctors underestimate the impact grief has on us, but many people get seriously ill or die soon after someone they love passes. It happens to old people all the time. It's not a coincidence.

I sensed him stroking my face as if trying to wipe away the tears. "Does that mean I'll be able to cross over and be with you soon? Because losing you has gutted me--there's nothing left inside, I'm just a hollow shell. Grief owns me. I don't think I can keep going on without you."

You have to. You still have things to do--we both do. We made an agreement together, before we came to earth, and we have to fulfill it. I've taken care of you, put you in a position where you don't have to worry about a thing.

"What agreement?"

Well, one thing, you need to teach other people about the afterlife, what it's really like. People are scared and confused about what's going to happen to them when they die. When their loved ones cross over they're devastated--they worry they'll never see them again. All that stuff about hell and damnation, it's not true. And no one ever dies, that's a misconception too.

We're made of energy and energy can't be destroyed. We just change form. You hear me and sense my presence, right?

"Yes," I answered.

Okay then, listen up. You're a writer--write a book. I'll tell you what to put in it.

CHAPTER 15

I knew Ron was right. Losing a person you love has to be one of the hardest thing any of us go through. Misunderstanding, fear, regrets, and guilt compound our suffering. Maybe I could help ease someone else's suffering by sharing my experiences and the wealth of information I'd gleaned in the process. The many books I'd read and the testimonies of other people had given me comfort. Perhaps it was my turn to give back.

Since Ron went home, I'd been keeping a journal of the things he told me and showed me about his life on the other side. I'd also saved the emails to and from his friends as well as my notes chronicling his time in the hospital. I had enough material to get started--and he'd promised to provide more. Writing might serve as therapy for me too.

• • •

Loneliness continued to permeate my days and nights, like a constant chill I couldn't chase away. Several months had elapsed since Ron's passing, but grief still sucked me down like quicksand. All these years he'd been an enormous presence in my life, the main focus of my thoughts, emotions, actions, goals, and hopes. I sometimes, teasingly, referred to him as the God of All That Mattered, but it was true for me. In most areas I'd deferred to him, allowing him to set my agenda and make decisions for me. Without his dynamic presence in my environment, keeping me alert and steering me in whatever direction he determined I needed to go, I felt uncertain and adrift. Nothing held meaning for me anymore, and I missed him with every cell in my body.

One Tuesday afternoon as I drove from our ranch into town to teach my weekly writing class--one of the few things I still enjoyed doing--I heard him singing a variation of an old Dan Hicks' song. *How can you miss me if I don't go away?* I smiled in spite of my glum mood.

By now you should realize I'm here with you all the time, he reminded me. *Even when you're not aware of my presence, I'm with you. We can't be separated, even if we wanted to be. Everything in the universe is part of a great Oneness that encompasses all that is, all that ever was, and all that will ever be. Like a spider web stretching into infinity with each strand tied to the others. The slightest touch at any part of the web, no matter how distant, sends ripples through the whole that can be sensed by everything else in the web.*

I'd studied metaphysical subjects long enough to be familiar with this concept. Yet it seemed I wandered aimlessly and alone in what I perceived as a wasteland, a vast emptiness that my friends, work, and activities couldn't fill.

Each so-called death you witness in this lifetime echoes previous deaths in other lifetimes, Ron

110

explained. *Each new wound rips off the scab of an older wound, leaving it raw and sore. About 600 earth years ago, you and I were orphaned sisters living in Scotland as servants in a manor house. Despite the beauty of our surroundings, our lives were bleak and hard. We rarely got to go outside, except to hang laundry or work in the garden. We endured harsh treatment from our employers, back-breaking toil, and a total lack of freedom or respect. The lady of the manor was very strict. If something didn't meet her standards we both got beatings. That's why I was such a perfectionist as Ron. I was a few years older than you, and you looked to me for protection and guidance. When I died of pneumonia at sixteen, you were left alone and helpless.*

I remembered the lifetime of which Ron spoke. I recalled the seemingly endless expanse of woodwork I'd polished, the floors I'd scrubbed, the damp, bone-chilling cold and the long winter nights when a bitter wind screamed across the heath like a wrathful demon. My sister and I slept in a cramped closet, huddled together for warmth, our stomachs growling with hunger. She was my protector, my compass, and the only thing that mattered to me in that forlorn existence. When she died I felt abandoned with no recourse, and died soon afterward.

Then in America, after the Civil War, you were a boy who traveled with a wagon train from Maryland bound for the Midwest, Ron continued. *I was your father then. We never reached our destination. Along the way, many of our group--including me--contracted smallpox and died. You were the last one left alive, but you couldn't survive in the wilderness by yourself and died alone.*

As he recounted the past-life agonies we'd endured together, I began to understand how those long-ago events had played a part in my present feelings of loss, sorrow, abandonment, and helplessness. The loneliness I now struggled with wasn't only due to natural grief over the passing of my beloved partner in this lifetime, it was rooted in sadness and desperation from having lost him again and again in centuries past.

• • •

In the mid-1980s, I became intrigued with the idea of reincarnation and regression, and decided to give it a try as research for a book I was editing. Since then, I've been regressed by a few professional therapists and undertaken the journey into the past on my own many times. Several psychics have described my previous incarnations too, and I've experienced instantaneous recall of earlier personalities.

I contemplated Ron's description of death as a revolving door through which we moved from one existence to another. We entered each life as we might enter a department store filled with myriad possibilities and choices. Each incarnation was a shopping trip to collect experiences. We selected lifetimes that looked interesting or that might help us develop qualities we sought, such as courage, patience, humility, strength, or compassion.

In *Illuminating the Afterlife,* Cindi Dale writes that we also incarnate to "allow the soul to manifest its spiritual purpose and to heal its soul wounds." Researchers such as Dr. Brian Weiss have discovered that physical injuries suffered during previous embodiments can cause infirmities, ailments, or scars in our current bodies. Weiss found that past-life regression could alleviate both physical and emotional problems. By healing old wounds from prior life traumas, we can release deeply ingrained fears and gain freedom.

One of my soul's wounds, it seemed, was loneliness that resulted from losing someone I loved--a wound Ron carried in his most recent life too, due to the death of his twin brother. Had he chosen to leave earth before me in this and other lifetimes because he feared losing me too?

When I first began looking into reincarnation, I had derived comfort from knowing the soul continued on after the body died. The promise of being reborn and reuniting with the people I loved here on earth at some time in the future gave me hope. Now, however, after having visited the wondrous place that awaits us when we shuck off our physical bodies, I longed to remain there forever. The idea of returning to earth again filled me with dread. I just wanted to finish what I'd come to do in this lifetime and leave here as soon as possible. I wanted to get whatever I'd come into this "store" to get, walk though that revolving door, and go home.

CHAPTER 16

I recalled the multicolored sea of souls I'd seen when I visited the place Ron called home, all bobbing and shimmering in an endless expanse of love. They didn't appear to be *doing* anything, though. Ron had spoken to me about undergoing his life review, but at some point he'd complete that. What happened next?

"What do you do over there?" I asked, as I packed a suitcase for a trip to visit my mother. Along with my own clothes, I tucked in a purple knit top I thought she might like (purple was her favorite color), plus a new mystery novel I might read to her if she felt up for hearing it.

I take care of you, and other people on earth, he answered. *I visit my old friends.*

Ron had friends throughout the States and around the world--some he'd known for five decades. He'd always been a traveler and had journeyed to every continent except Antarctica. Every year, he visited his many pals in Hawaii, as well as his longtime friends Louie, in Switzerland, and Karin, in Sweden. Only months before his passing, he'd gone back to the Pennsylvania town where he'd grown up for a class reunion with his old schoolmates.

Traveling is a lot easier now, he told me. *All I have to do is think of someplace and I'm there. No plane reservations to make, no packing, no security check-ins or waiting lines. I can even be in two places at once--a dozen places at once.*

"Sounds great," I said, thinking about the five-hour drive I'd make tomorrow to see my mother and a trip in August to visit friends in Massachusetts, where Ron and I lived before moving to Texas.

I'm still guiding planes too. Now I work through human controllers and pilots, giving them directions. Of course, they don't know that. When you fly back to Boston I'll be in charge. I can take much better care of you now than I could when I lived on earth.

"How does that work?" I asked.

I tap into people's minds and slip them information. You know how you sometimes get a sudden "aha" or a hunch or seem to know the answer to something you didn't realize you knew? It's probably one of us souls feeding you ideas. A lot of us over here do that, often in your dreams. We can insert ourselves into your dreams and influence the course they take. Our input has helped bring about most of the great inventions and advances on earth.

I thought about Edgar Cayce, aka the "Sleeping Prophet" who, while in trance, diagnosed illnesses and recommended cures for thousands of people, even though he'd had no medical training. In a sleep-like state, he psychically downloaded information from the spirit realm. Brilliant men and women through the ages, such as Elias Howe who invented the lock-stitch sewing machine, also came to mind. Howe claimed he'd gotten the idea in a dream.

Sometimes what seem to be accidents or mistakes are actually the results of us here tweaking people's designs, Ron continued.

Over the years people had "accidentally" stumbled upon many serendipitous innovations they hadn't set out to invent, including X-rays, stainless steel, Velcro, microwave ovens, and Post-it notes. How many of those bumbling inventors had been guided by spirits on the other side?

We're always creating, experimenting with ideas that haven't yet been tried in the physical world. All we have to do is imagine something and presto, it appears.

"Are you going to alter our world?"

Actually, we're altering it constantly. One of the benefits of working things out over here is we can see the results instantly, so we know immediately if something's not right. We don't have to invest a lot of time, money, and effort into a project that's ultimately going to fail. But that doesn't mean we always know the answers. We face challenges here, too, just like people do on earth. That's part of what makes it exciting.

He sounded so cheerful and enthusiastic, I put aside my own sadness momentarily so I could share in his happiness. "What have you invented so far?"

Well, nothing yet. I've only been here a little while and I've had a lot of other things to do since I got here. I'm thinking about designing a stabilizing device that will keep airplanes from bouncing around when they hit air turbulence.

"That sounds like a good idea," I said, wishing such a device could be installed before my upcoming trip to Boston. "How will I know if something I come upon is your invention?"

Oh, I'll be sure to let you know so you can invest in it at the get-go and make a gazillion dollars. I heard him chuckle. *Hey, remember your friend Jocelyn who died of ovarian cancer? She's creating new species of flowers now.*

I recalled how much Jocelyn loved flowers, how her garden always flourished. The thought of her designing flowers that might blossom one day on earth made me smile.

We test our ideas here in a sort of supernatural laboratory, Ron explained. *If something turns out well, we project it to people on earth in the form of epiphanies. We guide them through a series of "coincidences" to accomplish what needs to be done. That can be laborious and frustrating for us, but gradually humans get it and start to implement the ideas we send them.*

"It sounds like we're just puppets on strings."

Not really. Nobody forces you to follow our guidance--most people don't. You always have freedom to do what you want, even if it's counterproductive.

When he was on earth, Ron regularly told me what to do and how to do it. He gave me instructions on everything from driving to chopping vegetables to making financial investments. Often I rebelled against his bossiness, only to realize too late that he'd been right. From now on, I promised myself, I'd pay more attention and heed his advice.

• • •

The next day I drove to my mother's house on Lake Whitney, south of Dallas. I liked taking the back roads through wide open expanses of Texas country where I encountered little traffic--the complete opposite of the nerve-wracking "combat driving" and road rage that prevailed in the Boston area where I'd lived for thirty-one years.

I sensed Ron sitting in the seat beside me, guiding me as he'd promised. *Look around and tell me what you see,* he said.

"Cedar trees, cactus, rocks. A whole lot of empty space."

It's not empty. Hundreds of thousands of beings are out there.

"Of course, but I can't see all the little animals and lizards and insects."

I meant the spirits of people, like me, who used to live here, but also plant spirits and animal spirits. If we all had bodies it would look like Calcutta.

119

"Why are they here?" I asked.

Taking care of things on earth--earth needs a lot of help these days. Without them, the planet would become a lifeless shell.

The early Greeks, I recalled, believed every tree had a spirit called a dryad living in it and nymphs inhabited every body of water. These entities animated their hosts and served as nature guardians. Indigenous people of North America consider earth to be sacred, imbued with spirit, and teach that nonphysical animal guides live among us. Even though I couldn't see the spirits Ron described, I felt certain they were there.

About a hundred miles south of the town where my mother lived I stopped for gas. Again, the memory of the glowing orbs that populated the realm Ron called home flashed in my mind. Apparently, earth teemed with spirits too.

There are infinitely more souls than there are bodies to host them, Ron commented.

"Thank goodness," I said as I filled my Toyota's gas tank. "The planet's crowded enough as it is--nearly eight billion of us here, and growing."

As I replaced the nozzle in its cradle and waited for my receipt, I glanced down at the ground. Between my feet lay a shiny, pink pebble. I picked it up and turned it around in my hand: a piece of tumbled rose quartz. Climbing back into my car, I set the quartz crystal on the dashboard.

I put it there for you, Ron said.

"You can do that?"

Of course. Manifestation is the result of thought. Remember what I told you about how we create here with imagination? I'll explain more about that later.

I touched the stone again. According to people who work with crystals, rose quartz embodies the energy of love. "Thank you, darlin'."

• • •

Spending time with my mother always challenged my patience. She'd never been easy to get along with, but now that she was in her eighties and suffered from back pain, arthritis, and heart problems, she'd grown more irritable and demanding. Several small strokes had impaired her cognitive functioning, and her conversation rambled; sometimes she dozed off in mid-sentence. Usually I cut my visits short. After a couple days doing cooking, cleaning, running errands, and entertaining her as best I could I reached my limit.

On the drive back home, I chastised myself for my lack of compassion. Ron said kindness was important. Silently, I uttered a "thank you" to her husband who treated her with a great deal more kindness than I could muster.

Seeing my mother so frail, bent, and incapable of doing much of anything for herself, I knew I'd done the right thing in taking Ron off life support. Neither he nor I would have wanted him to exist in such a decrepit state--and if his doctors were right, Ron's fate would have been much, much worse than Mom's.

In the end, Ron's transition had been reasonably quick and easy, compared to the long, drawn-out, painful deaths many people endure. If only we had the option of granting our loved ones a peaceful passing, as we do our pets, we could alleviate so much suffering. The idea of "death with dignity" was gradually gaining acceptance, yet widespread fear of the unknown plus antiquated religious beliefs continued to throw up barriers.

Like Ron, I struggled with the fear of becoming incapacitated and dependent on others to care for me. Without children or a life partner, I might end up relying on the kindness of strangers in my final days on earth.

As I entered the town of Fredericksburg, twenty-some miles north of our ranch, I heard Ron reiterating something he'd told me before: *No one dies one moment earlier or later than he chooses.* Ron had chosen to go home in his own time and in his own way. My mother would too. And so would I.

CHAPTER 17

From my office window, I watched two workmen rip out the rotting, forty-year-old split-rail fence around what I still considered "our" house. The more progress they made, the more it seemed irrelevant to me. Why was I investing money in material things that didn't matter? I felt like a shopper buying stuff in a futile attempt to fill an emotional void.

After reading about, exploring, and listening to Ron's wondrous descriptions of the afterlife, I should have been content, knowing that he was at peace, that my own future with him on the other side was assured, and that all was well. Yet more than ever, I longed to "shuffle off this mortal coil" as Shakespeare called it in *Hamlet.*

I know you're not happy living on earth--I wasn't happy there either after my brother passed over, I heard Ron say.

I sensed him standing behind me, looking over my shoulder as if mentally directing the workers. This was the first project I'd undertaken alone to improve the property. I wondered how he felt about the choices I'd made to build a new cedar fence and a stone patio in the back of the house. If he were still here physically, he would have handled these decisions. Now I had only my own judgment to rely on.

You accepted this mission for your own growth and to help others, he continued, without mentioning my concerns about the fence or the patio. *You need to stay in a physical body for the time being, because it's easier for you as a human to tell other people about the things I'm showing you--and part of my job is to share information about what lies beyond earth. Actually, a lot of us here are eager to talk to you about the so-called afterlife. They love you too, baby, and trust you to present what they tell you as accurately as you can.*

I'd first read about so-called "death compacts" in Ian Currie's book *You Cannot Die.* According to him, the files of the British Society for Psychical Research, founded in England in 1882, contain many accounts of people who'd agreed that the first one who passed over would contact those who remained behind on earth.

"Imagine that you are now dead," Currie wrote. "What's the first thing you want to do? Tell those who are closest to you, of course."

Unfortunately, the people the deceased want to contact may not be ready, willing, or able to receive the messages their loved ones send them. Therefore, spirits may seek out mediums, psychics, or other sensitive individuals to serve as messengers.

One of the best-known and most amazing examples of spirit communication is that of Dr. Frederic Myers, a Cambridge University professor who founded the

Society and left his body in 1901. In an attempt to prove that souls really did live on after physical death, that they could communicate from the other side, and that mediums weren't just fabricating messages from departed spirits, Myers devised an experiment--a puzzle, really--he enacted from beyond the grave. His "compact" involved a number of intuitive individuals in various parts of the world. After his passing, he sent each person a piece of the puzzle that made no sense by itself. Only when each snippet was integrated with the pieces he slipped through the veil to the other intuitives in the group did Dr. Myers's words come together in a comprehensive way.

For more than thirty years, between 1901 and 1932, Myers diligently continued to communicate from the spirit realm with his colleagues on earth. During that time he conveyed more than 3,000 "scripts," an effort he found quite challenging.

"The nearest simile I can find to express the difficulties of sending a message," he transmitted in one attempt, "is that I appear to be standing behind a sheet of frosted glass--which blurs sight and deadens sound--dictating feebly--to a somewhat reluctant and obtuse secretary."

Had I made such a compact with Ron to fulfill a similar role? Did he struggle, as Myers did, to get through to an obtuse secretary? It seemed to me that I heard Ron's words and sensed his presence near me much of the time. Perhaps the intimate and emotional nature of our relationship made it easier for us to communicate than it had been for Myers to chat with his colleagues. But how could I know what information I *wasn't* picking up?

• • •

What did the souls on the other side want to tell me about the afterlife? And who were they? According to Ron, I had eleven souls in my inner circle; he had twenty-one. Were these the spirits who would seek me out to be their mouthpiece?

A medium I'd consulted, a woman known as "The Angel Lady," said each person on earth has at least seven spirit guides watching over him or her at all times. She referred to them as angels. For many years I'd known about my primary guardian Grace, as well as a secondary guide named Kailleagh and the two blithe and youthful spirits I called Megan and Moriah.

These beings spoke to me regularly and often made their presence known, especially when I was driving-- Grace occupied the passenger seat and the others sat in the back, where the "girls" cut up like human kids. However, I got the opinion these entities were of a different category than my "inner circle." Grace no longer incarnated and Megan and Moriah had never occupied physical bodies.

"Are our guides parts of ourselves, operating at a higher dimension?" I asked Ron one afternoon as I watered the plants that bordered the new patio. I found it easy to communicate with him while I did mundane tasks that put me into an almost meditative state.

Years ago, I'd read about a spiritual belief system called Huna. Attributed to the native Hawaiians, its concepts were popularized in the West in the mid-1900s by Max Freedom Long. It described three interconnected levels of consciousness or parts of a person. The intuitive, subconscious self is called the unihipili; the conscious, rational self is known as uhane; and the aumakua is said to be the divine aspect.

No, Ron answered, *they're distinct entities. They're your guardians, and mainly they protect you during your stay on earth. They're sort of like ancestors or relatives--in some cases they may have been relatives during earth lifetimes. Your grandmother in this go-round is one of your guides now and she'll continue watching over you until she reincarnates.*

I had fond memories of my maternal grandmother, even though she left earth when I was only thirteen. "Are my guides the same as the souls in my inner circle?"

No, although for some people and in some instances there may be some overlap. Souls in your inner circle can pitch in and protect you, too, the way I'm doing now. It's hard to explain. The members of your inner circle are more like dear friends, whom you want to be with always--and will. That's why you often incarnate together. You may incarnate as relatives, as Terry and I did, and as you and I have in many lifetimes. But your relatives aren't necessarily members of your inner circle. Your grandmother isn't part your circle and neither are your parents from this lifetime. You're more likely to pick your parents and grandparents for other reasons, perhaps to provide the body you want or the domestic circumstances you grow up in.

He must have noticed me frowning because he said, *I know it's confusing. Guides, guardians, however you want to think of them, come and go. Your primary guides will always be with you, but others might sign on for a particular task or for a period of time, the way your grandmother is doing now.*

My grandmother's husband had died suddenly of a heart attack before I was two years old; at the time she was younger than I was when Ron passed. Is that why she decided to step in and help me now, I wondered?

You can call on others when you need them, Ron said, *or Grace will do that--sort of like hiring temporary backup staff. Then there are spirits who influence you, even though you're not in direct contact with them. Some of them are responsible for large groups of beings, both physical and nonphysical.*

"Sounds like a lot of helpers for one woman." I laughed, remembering what he'd said about me never being alone.

You have no idea.

CHAPTER 18

Spirits make themselves known to us in various ways. Often they visit us in our dreams or in a shadowy half-conscious state between sleep and waking. I frequently smell scents that have no physical source or hear the tinkling of tiny bells where no bells exist.

Seeing spirits is known as clairvoyance. Hearing them is called clairaudience. The term clairsentience means sensing them with your body, like the feeling I get of Ron stroking my hair. In an uncommon type of perception called synesthesia, a person blends two or more senses, so that you may hear colors or taste sounds.

Many people experience peculiar activity involving electronics, especially electric lights and computers, which paranormal researchers attribute to spirits. Ron sometimes plays around with my computer, running slideshows or videos that contain meaningful photos on my monitor. He also fiddles with lights. During the funeral of a friend's father, a decorated World War II pilot whom Ron admired, the chandelier above my head blinked continuously throughout the service and I knew Ron had come to pay his respects. My friend Sylvia, who's a medium, noted that the lights in her house flicker repeatedly when she does readings for me, though they behave normally at other times.

One afternoon Lyndsey and I were using a Ouija board, trying to connect with someone on the other side. Ron had already refused to talk through the board-- spelling out a message letter by letter was way too laborious for him. Suddenly one of the overhead lights in my living room began rapidly blinking on and off, and I sensed him laughing.

Spirits use other tactics to get our attention too. My friend Claire lives in an antique saltbox house built in the 1690s--it's one of the oldest existing residences in the U.S. In 2009, Claire's mother died peacefully in the house at the age of 101. When I'm there, I often hear her mother calling my name loud and clear. I also hear footsteps on the wooden floor of the house's second story, even when no one else is at home. I keep hoping one day she'll play Claire's beautiful Steinway piano that formerly belonged to her and to her own mother.

During the summer of 2014, two of my Texas friends visited me while I was staying in Claire's house. Neither of them believed in spirits. However, at night one of them saw a ghostly figure of a woman cross through her bedroom and the other heard someone walk from the doorway to her bedside. A carpenter, who was replacing windows in the house, reported seeing the elderly woman many times. To me it seemed she was checking out these people she didn't know who were hanging around her house to make sure everything was okay.

Such an old house has probably witnessed a lot of deaths, births, and other important events. One night my friend Lyndsey stayed there, but got very little sleep. "It seemed like a party was going on in the bedroom," she said in the morning. She'd sensed the presence of many people in the room with her--one even sat on the bed and pushed her shoulder, as if urging her to get up and join in the fun. Could the spirits of former residents have been celebrating the birth of a baby in that bedroom or preparing a bride for her wedding?

It's important to remember that spirits who present themselves to us--in whatever manner--rarely mean to frighten or harm us. Usually they're friends or loved ones who've come to assure us that they're fine, they're still with us, and they still love us.

In her book *Visits from the Afterlife,* medium Sylvia Browne makes a distinction between spirits and ghosts. Spirits, she writes, are beings who have transitioned from the physical world to our joyful home beyond earth. Ghosts are souls who've gotten stuck here, instead of moving into the light of the afterlife--they may not even realize they're "dead" and might wonder why no one pays any attention to them.

A documentary titled *Calling Earth,* produced by Dan Drasin in 2013, presents some of what I consider the most intriguing evidence of spirit communication. In it, a team of researchers, scientists, and academics actually recorded the voices of people who no longer live on earth, including the Latvian psychologist Dr. Konstantin Raudive. While he was still in human form, Raudive recorded 7,000 voice texts of disincarnate beings. The practice is known as ITC, or instrument transcommunication. The results of his experiments were published in 1971, in a book titled *Breakthrough: An Amazing Experiment in Electronic Communication with the Dead.*

Drasin's documentary also chronicles a five-year-long study (1993-1998) in Norfolk, England called the Scole Experiment. During their experiment, Scole's researchers captured numerous manifestations of spirit activity, including "messages" from the other side in the form of images on 35-millimeter camera film--film still sealed inside its metal canister and secured in a padlocked box.

My purpose for writing this book is not to convince skeptics that our souls continue living after our physical bodies die, or that our deceased loved ones can and do communicate with us from the afterlife. However, you may find it interesting to delve into some of the extensive scientific research that's been conducted over more than a century--there's so much, in fact, that you may come to the same decision I did. It's more ludicrous to disbelieve than to believe in life after death.

• • •

Since ancient times, people have conceived of spirit animals that guide and protect human beings. Legends also talk about mortal shamans who can shapeshift into animals and birds, and who journey between the material and spirit realms.

A medium I consulted shortly after Ron went home told me Ron would send a male cardinal to let me know whenever he was nearby. One morning I was awakened by something banging incessantly on my bedroom window. Grudgingly I opened my eyes and saw a bright red cardinal hammering his wings against the glass and pecking at it noisily. He kept up the racket until I got out of bed and looked through the window at him.

"Hi there," I said to the bird, realizing Ron had sent him.

Soon cardinals began to visit me regularly. Often they perched in the tree outside my office window. Sometimes the birds sat on a windowsill or on the new cedar fence that runs in front of my house. At dusk I frequently saw a flash of red darting between the trees and knew Ron is saying goodnight.

Then, for a time, no cardinals appeared. I missed them. Did their absence mean Ron had left me? Eventually, however, they began turning up in unexpected places. Facebook friends posted pictures of cardinals in their yards. I'd helped organized a dance for peace at a church in my town; one of the presenters showed up wearing cardinal earrings. Someone left a notepad and a calendar illustrated with cardinals in my mailbox at the continuing education center where I teach.

Finally, one afternoon a beautiful red bird landed on the windowsill outside my office. "Hi Ron," I said. "I'm happy you're here."

I'd just logged into Facebook and noticed a post with a link from my medium friend Sylvia. It turned out to be a music video called "Forever Country," produced by Sky Arts, a collaboration of artists singing a medley of tunes made popular by artists such as John Denver, Willie Nelson, and Dolly Parton.

I watched the video in amazement, not only for the music but because of the background scenery (which had little to do with the songs and which critics had panned as "frenetic"). Throughout the video trees, buildings, fences, railroad tracks, and rock formations continually rose, evolved, disintegrated, and morphed magically--the way I imagined they did in Ron's world when souls there tried out their creations. *We're always creating over here,* he'd told me, *experimenting with ideas. All we have to do is imagine something and presto, it appears.*

I thought about how he sang to me now to express things he'd found difficult to talk about when he was still human. Now that he was no longer embodied, he'd said, *I can use anyone else's voice to talk to you.* And so he had. At the end of the video, Dolly Parton, wearing a white gown that made her look like an angel, sang one of my favorite songs "I Will Always Love You" and I knew Ron was letting her speak for him.

I heard him chuckle. *I'm glad you got that. It took some effort to pull it all together.*

With tears in my eyes, I said, "I will always love you too, darlin'."

CHAPTER 19

The Moravian Book Shop in Bethlehem, Pennsylvania, where I lived in the early 1970s and about an hour north of the town where Ron grew up, is the oldest continuously operating bookstore in the world. This delightful store is housed in an antique building in the city's historic district. Reputedly, the bookstore is haunted. Members of the shop's staff say they've seen a shadowy woman dressed in white as well as a "kitchen ghost" who hangs out in the basement and snitches supplies (though he returns them if asked).

Spirits exist among humans all the time, but most of us don't notice them while we go about our everyday business. Or, if we do, we usually don't talk about it. Contacts are often so subtle we miss them if we're not prepared to believe in such stuff. Perhaps spirits don't want to frighten us, therefore they rarely burst into our lives with a lot of fanfare that might shock us. Maybe, as Cambridge University Professor Frederic Myers lamented, it's really hard for disembodied entities to get through to us dense earthlings. Their gentle touch and soft voices can easily be overlooked, explained away as birdsong or wind or distant music emanating from an unidentifiable source.

I consider myself lucky to be able to experience regular contact with nonphysical entities--Ron most of all, but with others too. The "messages" I receive and their purposes vary in type, but always prompt a sense of "aha" that lets me know someone is trying to get my attention.

Usually they're little things. One day, for example, I picked up a notepad to jot down a few thoughts for a book I was writing and a photo of Ron slipped from between the pages. I didn't recall ever having seen that particular photo before--it was probably taken thirty years ago--and I certainly hadn't tucked it in the notepad. I interpreted it as a signal that Ron wanted to let me know he'd stopped by to say "Hi."

On another occasion, while I was sitting in my car waiting for a friend, I decided to listen to some music on my cell phone. I touched the Pandora icon that should have brought me a Celtic tune, but instead Ron's voice came through--he'd redirected my phone to a two-year-old recorded message he'd left for me while he was still embodied.

As I discussed in the previous chapter, spirits like to play around with electronic devices. After watching the documentary *Calling Earth*, which chronicled a group of researchers who recorded the voices of disincarnate entities, I attempted to capture Ron's voice on my cell phone. I tried consistently for several weeks, without success. Then one day as I'd replayed half an hour of dead air, the phone suddenly skipped of its own volition to a reading with a medium that I'd recorded months ago. I heard her say, "He's still here."

Sometimes spirits contact us through other people, especially if we aren't open to their attempts. Mediums and psychics aren't the only channels they choose for communication. A friend or relative or even a stranger may convey, perhaps unwittingly, a message from an entity who's on the other side. That's what happened on the day after Ron left his physical body, when he made his presence known to the daughter of my friend Claire because I was too distraught at the time for him to get through to me directly.

On a number of occasions, spirits have come to me during Reiki sessions. I sense the guardian angels and departed loved ones of the people I'm working on-- they stop by to visit and sometimes assist me in the process. I see them bending over the person lying on the massage table or feel them standing beside me, laying their hands over mine. Reiki, a healing modality that taps the energy of love, brings both practitioner and patient into a place of peace, compassion, and receptivity.

One afternoon my friend and teacher, Anne, who'd given Reiki to Ron during his transition to the afterlife, was working on me when she heard him insist she let me know he was there with us.

"I heard him say 'Skyebird, Skyebird' repeatedly," she told me.

I believe what he really said was "Skyeperson," a nickname he gave me early in our relationship. I'm named for the Isle of Skye in Scotland, and the island's natives are known as Skyepersons. However, Anne didn't know about this endearment.

During another Reiki session I smelled the luscious scent of roses mixed with gardenias, even though the fragrance had no physical source. Roses, of course, represent love. The ancient Greeks believed gardenias transported a person to the heavenly realm, where all is sweet and joyful. They also symbolize renewal, hope, enlightenment, understanding, trust, clarity, intuition, insight, protection, and inner peace.

One Saturday I decided to go horseback riding. I live on a cooperative ranch and my neighbors and I own about a dozen horses collectively. Hired wranglers take care of the horses and organize group trail rides for residents and their guests. When I showed up at the stables on that salubrious afternoon, I was amused and delighted to find that I'd been assigned to ride a horse named Hollywood--Ron's nickname.

Occurrences such as these aren't unique or in any way outstanding. In fact, communications like these are common and happen all the time. An extensive body of literature exists about interactions between spirits and humans, and includes many awe-inspiring examples far more intriguing than mine.

Spirits can be amazingly creative in their attempts to contact us. Don't discount experiences that may be less dramatic than what the saints and mystics have reported--your encounters may be equally important.

Perhaps if we can accept that ordinary people like me can and do have contact with beings in other realms of existence, we'll find it easier to recognize and understand what our loved ones in the afterlife are trying to tell us.

• • •

Recently I'd read a book about crop circles, a phenomenon that's fascinated and bewildered people for many years. Although hoaxers form some circles, researchers point out a number of distinctions between the obviously manmade designs and the ones that defy explanation. The mysterious configurations, they say, tend to be more intricate in their proportions than the circles made by humans, and many incorporate sacred geometry.

The crop circles are generally completed quietly, unbeknownst to residents or neighbors, during a single, short summer night. These complex formations, if they were created by humans, would likely require a sizable construction crew, employing noisy equipment and bright lights to produce the designs within such a limited time frame. Furthermore, the grain stalks in manmade circles usually become broken during the process of tamping them down, whereas the stalks in the mysterious circles are merely bent.

"Do aliens make the ones scientists can't explain?" I asked Ron.

He laughed. *Well, not those little green guys in spaceships.*

"Who then?"

Spirits of various kinds. They visualize what they want to create, and then work with weather forces to produce results. Believe it or not, it's easier to manipulate weather than to get humans to do something.

"Sounds like something you'd enjoy, directing the weather to do your bidding." During his thirty-seven years as an air traffic controller, Ron had become an expert on weather and knew more about it than most meteorologists.

Nope, I've never participated in making one. My work with weather is of a different sort. You'd probably like making crop circles though.

I would indeed. I had a passion for labyrinths, stone circles, and other sacred-earth configurations. I'd spent six weeks during the spring of 1998 building a stone labyrinth in the woods behind my house in Gloucester, Massachusetts, and I walked it almost every day. Over the years, it attracted many fascinating people and a variety of nonphysical entities who have participated in my spiritual growth. In December of 2000, Ron and I visited Stonehenge and Avebury together, where we were filmed by the BBC for a Discovery Channel TV special called "Secret Stonehenge."

"What's the purpose of crop circles?" I asked.

Some circles are intended to convey information through their designs--it's a way to let humans know that other entities exist and are trying to make contact. But few people are sophisticated enough to understand the messages contained there. Sometimes spirits just have fun designing the formations--it's sort of a game. We enjoy creating things, you know. Maybe you'll get to see a "real" crop circle one day, but try not to get caught in the process of making one while you're still human. It can be pretty nerve-wracking. Wait until you come over to this side to do that.

CHAPTER 20

The night before I left for my trip to Massachusetts in the summer of 2013, I dreamt about Ron with another woman. While he was human, his flirtatious behavior had always been a burr under my saddle, as folks in Texas say. An exceptionally handsome man, he also possessed intelligence, charm, charisma, sophistication, athletic ability, good taste, generosity, and many other admirable qualities--plus he still exuded a bad-boy attitude along with an irrepressible self-confidence that had won him the affection of countless women over the years. Being an identical twin only added to his caché.

When I began exploring our past incarnations, I discovered this had been a theme in many of our prior lifetimes together. Even so, the combination of my insecurity and his commitment phobia in this life caused innumerable arguments between us. Loving Ron was like riding a spirited horse. I couldn't control him, all I could hope to do was hang on and enjoy the ride.

I dragged myself out of bed and into the bathroom. While I stood under the shower, still smarting from the dream and grumbling to myself, I sensed Ron beside me.

Jealousy and possessiveness don't exist over here, he said. *We're not dominated by our egos. Our purpose is to bring love and understanding to those of you on earth. By the way, that's your purpose too, baby.*

"What do you mean?"

Suddenly, I heard him singing the old Beatles' song "All You Need Is Love."

He shifted gears from the personal to the spiritual, and explained, *Here, where I am now, love is the natural order of things. We don't question it. On earth it's much harder to live love--notice how only the letter O separates those two words? The circle represents completion, wholeness, and unity. Human beings spend their entire lifetimes searching for love, but most of what we find is a parody of the real thing--and it causes us more pain than pleasure.*

I massaged shampoo into my hair while I waited for him to continue. After a few moments, during which I thought he'd left, he said, *Part of why we come to earth is to bring with us a spark of what we really are, and that spark is love. I don't mean infatuation or romance or desire. I'm talking about unconditional love, the force that creates and enlivens all life on earth and unites all beings in the universe. What you experienced during your brief visit here. People like you, Skye, who know the truth, need to tell others. You have a responsibility to help people remember that love is all that matters. It's the only thing that's real.*

I shut off the water and stepped out of the shower. "It sounds strange to hear you say that," I said as I toweled myself dry. "I know you loved me and your friends and your brother. But you were angry at pretty much everyone else and at the world in general. It seemed like you hated more than you loved. Forgive me, darlin', but right now you sound like a 1960s flower child."

I sensed him nod in agreement. *You're right. Anger and bitterness ruled me, and that interfered with my ability to love. When souls decide to come to earth, we fully intend to bring love into a confused world, but after we actually incarnate we forget. That pink light you saw over here gets blocked by shadows when you're inside a human body. Instead of making things better, I was making things worse during those last years of my life. My batteries had run down and I needed to recharge them. I needed to plug into the force of love again. I'm doing that now.*

"So what am I supposed to do? How can I 'live love' when the love of my life is gone?"

First of all, I'm not "gone." You know better. I'm here with you right now. Now and always.

"I'm working on accepting that," I said, pulling on a T-shirt and jeans.

Next, try to remember that people who can't love-- or think they can't because they're overwhelmed by fear, loneliness, and hatred--need love most, even though they make it nearly impossible for other people to love them.

"That may be true, but I don't see what I can do about it."

147

You didn't stop loving me when I behaved badly, even when I pushed you away.

"But I couldn't have stopped loving you no matter what. I can't do that with total strangers."

Love flows from the highest to the lowest places, the way water does. You can't imagine how much love is flowing to earth right this moment, how much love we're showering you with. The more you can connect with what we send from the higher realms, the more you can spread it around.

"I'll try," I muttered, unconvinced.

Let me show you something pretty, baby, something inside you. Close your eyes and turn your attention to the center of your chest, near your heart. Notice a light shining there?

I closed my eyes and leaned against the bathroom vanity. I focused my inner sight on my fourth chakra. "Okay, I see it. It's about the size of an orange."

Let it expand until it fills your entire torso. Instead of feeling emptiness and loss, let this light fill you and bring you peace.

After a few moments I said, "Yes, I can feel it and see it. It's green."

This connects you to the spirit world. Now imagine radiating the light out into the world, as if you were a lighthouse shining a beam into the darkness.

The chakras, as I understood them, serve as portals through which light-energy flows from higher realms into our physical bodies.

Regardless of where you go, you can follow this beam of light back here, back to your home.

"You mean I can come there and be with you?"

Eventually, but not yet. I just want you to know that you have a home here forever. This may be hard for you to grasp because you never knew a loving home on earth. But what I'm showing you now is true. You hold a piece of this true home inside you all the time. You brought it with you when you incarnated. Part of you is still over here too. You're like those lighthouses up and down the New England coastline, and you can shine a powerful, life-saving beam into the darkness to bring others ashore. It's up to you to tell other people and show them the way back home.

"How can I do that? I'm not even sure I believe all this myself."

I'll teach you. That's an agreement you and I made together.

● ● ●

Flowers are one of the myriad things I missed since moving from Massachusetts to Texas. In the spring, wildflowers spread across the Texas Hill Country like colorful patchwork quilts--sapphire bluebonnets, red Indian paintbrush, yellow coreopsis, and pink primrose. But when summer comes, the blazing heat burns everything golden-brown. Unless you've trucked in good soil and watered constantly, you can't expect to grow much the rest of the year.

While sitting on my friend Claire's patio in the nearly four-hundred-year-old fishing community of Gloucester, Massachusetts, I let my gaze roam over the many flowers that clustered around the house, edged the driveway, and blossomed in the shade beneath eighty-foot-tall locust trees. In early June, those locusts bloomed with fragrant ivory flowers that made me think of bridal veils, but I was too late to enjoy them this year. I'd missed the luscious scent of spring lilacs, too, and the jellybean-hued azaleas. In the pretty, nearby town of Rockport, multicolored annuals grew in window boxes on antique cottages, unmolested by the hungry deer that gobbled up everything in the heart of Texas.

I thought about my friend Jocelyn, whom Ron said now developed new types of flowers. I hoped she'd come up with some gorgeous species that deer didn't eat and that could thrive in poor, rocky soil with little water.

Ron had always liked Claire and her husband Joel, who'd died from brain cancer in 2004. We'd spent many happy times with them before moving to Texas, so I wasn't surprised that Ron had chosen to hang out here with me during my first visit back since his passing.

Look at the roses growing on the trellis near the front door, Ron said. *What do you see?*

"Pink roses. Is this a trick question?"

Ignoring my comment, he continued, *Now close your eyes and try to sense their life force, the spirit that animates the roses.*

150

"How?" I asked.

Remember when I showed you the light in your heart chakra? I want you to connect with that light and feel it expanding, reaching out like a lighthouse beam-- well, maybe just a flashlight beam considering they're only ten feet away--until it touches the roses.

With my eyes closed, I tried to imagine a gold-white glow within me, then to aim it at the flowers. After several moments passed a warm, tickling sensation began below my heart, as if a pleasant breeze were blowing across my stomach.

Okay, now open your eyes and look at the roses again.

"Oh," I cried, startled by how brilliantly they now shone in the morning sun. They seemed to be made of pure light instead of substance. No longer were they just pretty pink flowers--their vibrant colors sparkled and rippled and danced. As I continued gazing at them, I realized their radiant glow came from an inner source.

You're seeing the spirit in the roses. That's what animates them. And you're right, they are made of light. Everything is.

"They're so beautiful!"

The flowers over here are a thousand times more beautiful. Flowers, trees, animals--plus all kinds of things that don't exist on earth, as well as things that used to exist there but don't now. All made of light.

"When you look at earth, do you see the life force in all things, the way I saw it just a moment ago in the roses?"

Yes, but it's much more intense. Actually, I don't pay much attention to the surfaces of things, only their spirits. Now that you know how, you can do that too.

• • •

Following Ron's instructions, I practiced seeing light in things around me. Always, the light seemed joyful. Always it welcomed me, like a dear friend.

I found it relatively easy to see the life force in flowers and other plants. Water, too, shimmered with inner light, not only reflected sunshine. The water-filled quarry at Halibut Point State Park--one of my favorite spots on earth, about two miles from Claire's house-- offered a perfect setting for light-gazing. While sitting on a granite cliff about twenty feet high, I let my sight soften and looked slightly above the water's surface. A whitish glow rippled there, like a sparkling, swirling mist. Moiré in motion. Austrian psychiatrist and scientist Wilhelm Reich, in the middle of the last century, had observed and written about this life energy. He called it orgone.

Light emanated from trees too. Not only did I see their life force, I felt it pulsing, almost as if the trees purred. The few quartz crystals I'd brought with me on this trip gave off plenty of light and resonance. They effervesced like champagne when I held them, shooting out tiny "sparks" that I sensed might be a type of communication, if only I could comprehend the stones' language.

Dr. Richard Gerber, author of *Vibrational Medicine,* explained that the "physical universe is composed of orderly patterns of frozen light." That's not the way I saw it, however. From my perspective, the light undulated and glistened and sang.

CHAPTER 21

Why did I come to earth? What am I supposed to be doing here? We've all pondered these questions at some time in our lives. Even though everyone has the same, universal goal of dispelling fear through the power of love, our souls may take on embodiment for individual reasons too.

Sometimes we assume human forms in order to be with people we love who are already living on earth. Other times, we may incarnate to rectify or complete a situation that's rooted in another life experience. If our actions in one life have caused an imbalance, we may choose to return to set things right. Many spiritual teachers refer to earth as a "school" where we come to learn. In his book *Many Lives, Many Masters,* Brian L. Weiss, MD, reports that there are "different levels of learning, and we must learn some of them in the flesh. We must feel the pain. When you're a spirit you feel no pain."

Ron told me the same thing. *Life on earth is supposed to be hard. No pain, no gain. Part of the purpose of being physical is to experience pain and fear--those things don't exist over here. Learn not to participate in all that, not to cause it or let it overwhelm you. You grow by detaching from it and dealing with it constructively.*

I remembered reading butterflies must beat their wings against the inner walls of their cocoons to free themselves; through this struggle they become strong enough to fly. The dense energy of earth and the limitations of the corporeal body pose difficulties for the incarnating soul. When we enter human forms, we lose awareness of the immense love and light we knew while in the spirit world. Our vision narrows. We become immersed in the fear and darkness that prevail on earth. Apparently, this amnesia is necessary for us to meet the challenges facing us and to grow through coping with hardship.

In his book *Conversations with God,* however, Neal Donald Walsh proposes that we choose earth lives not to learn, but "To remember, and re-create, Who You Are." He writes "life is not a process of discovery, but a process of creation."

Gary Zukav, author of *The Seat of the Soul,* disputes the concept of "past lives." According to him, "From the point of view of the soul, all of its incarnations are simultaneous. All of its personalities exist at once. Therefore, the release of negativity that occurs in one of the soul's incarnations benefits not only itself, but all of its soul's other incarnations also."

After Ron left his physical body, I stepped up my attempt to understand these age-old questions. All of us have special talents and gifts to offer. I noticed that souls seemed to fall into certain categories according to their basic natures, their objectives, and the roles they played on earth (and elsewhere). With Ron's help, I identified several classifications or types of souls that included leaders, protectors, teachers, healers, warriors, artists, inventors, explorers, and caretakers, though I'm sure I missed some. If you trace your soul's "lineage" through a series of lifetimes, you'll probably notice a thread of continuity running through most of them. The details of the lives themselves will be different--a warrior soul may be a soldier in one lifetime and an athlete in another--but an underlying theme remains consistent.

I determined my soul's "role" is that of a teacher. In this lifetime, I've taught writing and interior design classes in colleges, adult ed classes, workshops, and other venues. I've also created mail-order courses in feng shui and astrology. A lot of my published books have a "self-help" angle, and my goal in writing them has been to convey information gleaned from my own studies and experiences, as well as the work of others.

When I plunged deeper into my sojourns on earth, a pattern stretching back thousands of years emerged. During one of my earliest memories, from sometime around 200 B.C.E., I worked as a slave in the library at Alexandria, Egypt. There I was exposed to knowledge and written words, but I never learned to read or write. In another incarnation as a nun in a convent, I served as a scribe copying manuscripts. My search uncovered a number of lifetimes as a nun--I'd repeatedly chosen a cloistered existence because in earlier times that offered one of the few opportunities for women to get an education.

It's not uncommon for souls to choose more than one role, and our incarnations may alternate between these. I've also had lifetimes as an artist and a healer. This time around, I've combined all three paths. Ron, I learned, has qualities of both a warrior and a leader soul.

As we go about expressing our souls' purposes, we find ways to reunite with members of our "inner circle" in order to further our own growth as well as theirs. Ron had talked to me about two previous lives we'd shared. I'd also regressed myself to another experience, an ancient incarnation when I was a gentle, dreamy boy who liked to draw pictures in the dirt, on stones, and on the walls of caves. In that lifetime Ron was my older brother, a powerful warrior and the leader of our small clan. Our existence in what's now the western part of Russia was hard, and we roamed the land with the animal herds we hunted for food.

One day we spotted another band of humans. My brother wanted to join forces with them, thinking to increase our chances of survival in such a harsh land. He dictated a message that I translated into symbols-- with a burned stick I drew the images on a piece of tree bark. When I delivered my brother's message of peace to a member of the other tribe, however, he bashed in my skull with a rock, killing me instantly. My death precipitated a bloody fight during which my brother and most of our clan died.

Now, I wanted to know more about who and what we'd been to each other in the past, and how those long-ago lifetimes had influenced the present. One evening I sat on a granite sea wall in Gloucester, Massachusetts, watching lobster boats chug their way home at the end of the day. The sun dipped low in the darkening sky and fingers of vermilion light stretched across the expanse of blue. The blue of Ron's eyes.

I sensed his presence beside me and said, "Tell me more about our past together."

Are you sure?

"I'm sure."

A long pause made me wonder if he was still there. Finally, he said, *I wish it were otherwise, but we haven't had many happy lifetimes together.*

"Why?" I asked.

Few people have happy lifetimes. Until recently, life on earth was pretty grim for most folks--hard work, poverty, disease--and they had few choices. Women bore the worst of it, subject to men's whims and the perils of childbirth. That's why in most of my lives I wanted to be a man.

"Is that why I never had children in this lifetime?"

Partly. Mostly, you and I have been family members. Once, in the late 1600s in Prussia, I was your mother and you were my cherished son. Although I had other children, I loved you the best. When you died of a respiratory illness at age two my heart broke.

"I can't imagine you as my mother," I said. "In my fantasies, you're always a king or at least a knight in shining armor."

And so I was, many times and in many parts of the world. In Scotland in what earth counts as the ninth century, I ruled as chieftain of a clan. You were the clan's wise woman. You healed people, concocted spells to ward off evil spirits, and foretold the future. Next to me, you were the most powerful person in the village. We respected each other, but disagreed about many aspects of village life. We were never lovers. You were much older than me and ugly by any standard-- and as chief I could take my pick of the pretty young women in the community. I had a wife and many children, but you chose to remain single and childless.

As he spoke, the sound of war drums pounded in my ears and I could smell the smoke of fires burning. I felt a twinge of fear.

Then the Nordic people invaded. Unfortunately, neither my powers nor yours could prevent them from plundering our village and murdering our people. Their superior numbers and weapons defeated us. I lost my left hand and suffered many other wounds in battle. My wife deserted me, seeing a better opportunity for herself and our children, and left our land in the company of an enemy warrior. You and I escaped to the Isle of Skye, where you ministered to me. You were content

*there, but I was a defeated man, a vanquished leader.
Despite your help I died, devastated.*

I thought about how arthritis and swelling in his left
wrist had plagued him for years. Could there be a
connection? Brian Weiss might say so.

I pressed him for more information. "What about
the other people you've been close to this time around?
How about your brother Terry? Did you know him in
previous lifetimes?"

He was the Nordic warrior who cut off my hand.

• • •

"Human life is a journey. It is not a prison sentence."

I'd just finished reading this passage in *Emmanuel's
Book III* when I heard Ron speaking. *Earth isn't bad,*
he said. *It's just limited and hard. Earth's energy is
dense and heavy. Dragging around a body is a lot of
work. You have to feed and clothe it, wash it, exercise it,
house it, fix it when it gets damaged--and you have to
work to make money to take care of all those things.
Even if it's a good body it's still a huge burden,
compared to the freedom we have over here.*

A picture of a horse wearing blinders and pulling a
heavy wagon flashed in my mind.

*Of course, there are things you can only enjoy in a
physical body. Sex, for instance.*

I contemplated the words of the eighteenth-century
Hasidic master Reb Hayim Haikel who suggested,
"Creation was for the purpose of lovemaking. As long
as there was only one-ness, there was no delight."

161

We don't come to earth only to learn through overcoming hardships, Ron continued. *We also come to explore. Souls are infinitely curious and we like to experiment with different things, including physical incarnation. We like to try out the ideas we've created, too, to see if they'll hold up under earth's rigorous conditions.*

"Like those flowers Jocelyn is designing?" I asked, wishing I could see my friend's creations.

Right. Much of what we imagine here won't survive, or not for long. By testing our ideas on earth we learn ways to improve on the original concepts.

"I thought with all your advanced knowledge and expanded perspective you'd already know what would work here and what wouldn't."

He chuckled. *What fun would that be? Souls often learn more during tough lifetimes than easy ones. The most painful or perilous episodes in our journeys through life may provide the greatest opportunities for growth. You sell yourself short if you shy away from challenges and take the easy road.*

I recalled a sculpture class I'd taken when I was a junior in college, a class I'd expected to sail through. When I got my midterm grade, I was shocked to see the professor had given me an F. Angrily, I confronted him, insisting I was the best student in the class. He replied he wasn't grading me against the others, he was grading me according to how well I'd fulfilled my ability.

Putting aside my righteous indignation, I redoubled my efforts. To my surprise, I enjoyed working harder and challenging myself to see what I could accomplish. I found it exciting to push beyond my former limits and discover new ways to deal with problems, instead of just coasting along. The results pleased me more than my earlier, half-hearted attempts and I felt proud of myself. At the end of the term, I received my well-deserved A.

Even short-term difficulties can be valuable to us, Ron continued. *My last days in the hospital, for instance. I'd always been such an independent person, always the guy in control. Suddenly I couldn't do anything for myself. I was totally reliant on other people to keep me alive. I had to allow you to make decisions for me--I had no say in the matter. As a result of that experience, I learned a much-needed lesson in patience, vulnerability, and trust. I learned to let go and let others take care of me. What I gained in those four days will benefit me when I return to earth.*

Remembering that heart-rending time, I teared up. Before I could dwell on those memories, though, Ron presented me with a more mind-boggling concept. *Some adventurous souls even choose to undertake two earth lives simultaneously.*

"What?" I exclaimed. "How is that possible?"

Physics. Everything is made up of energy, human beings as well as disincarnate souls. Energy can operate in more than one place at the same time. A particle can exist in numerous spaces, times, or dimensions at once.

Even when particles that were once connected are separated, they remain linked energetically--and if one changes the other does too.

"But why would a soul want to go through life in the bodies of two people?" The challenges of a single lifetime seemed, to me, daunting enough. I couldn't imagine how complicated it might be to undergo dual earthly existences concurrently.

To learn more and advance faster. In college you completed two majors simultaneously, and you often worked two jobs, sometimes three, at the same time. You wanted to pack in as much experience as you could.

As I mulled over the perplexing idea, I recalled an odd experience I'd had in Boston when I was in my late twenties. After work, I'd taken the subway home, as I did every weekday evening. In the crowded car I noticed a woman passenger who looked like me. Her hair was a little longer than mine and she was a couple inches taller, but otherwise we could have been twins. I don't have a twin; even my sisters and I don't look much alike. This strange woman, however, was my mirror image. Throughout the commute we kept glancing at one another--she must have been as surprised and confused as I was--but the packed subway car made it impossible for us to connect. I never saw her again. Was she my double on a soul level? Or were our mirror-image features merely a coincidence?

While contemplating the concept of simultaneous incarnations, I wondered what might happen if I encountered a person in whom my soul also resided (assuming I'd chosen to split myself into two bodies). Would I recognize the individual who shared my soul? Would I know we were, in the true sense of the term, kindred spirits? Would our paths in this lifetime be similar? And if so, what could I learn from this other human being who wasn't *other* at all, but someone who was traveling the path along with me in a mutual quest for wisdom?

CHAPTER 22

Four months after Ron's passing, I scattered some of his ashes in Gloucester's Folly Cove, a place that has held profound, even sacred meaning for me since 1988. This was my sanctuary, my holy place. I'd lived in an antique Cape Cod cottage overlooking this cove for seventeen years and spent countless hours sitting on the granite rocks above it, watching the tide ebb and flow as my life did. Whenever I had a problem, needed to think, or sought solace I came here.

Sometimes I combed the beach for sea glass; on a few occasions I swam in the icy water that even in August rarely got above 65 degrees. During the Perfect Storm of 1991 I'd stood on the bank above the cove, leaning into the wind with the rain lashing my face, as I watched waves as tall as my house slam the rocks and crash on the shore with a ferocity that humbled me in the face of nature's power. I'd loved this rugged crook at the north tip of Cape Ann's picturesque shoreline with a passion I'd never felt for a place before. Only my love for Ron could have pulled me away from the only home I'd ever known.

As I dribbled the powdery ashes into the water, I heard Ron say, *That's not me.*

"I know," I replied, tears running down my cheeks. "But us earthbound folks are sentimental about such things."

I felt his gentle touch stroking my hair. *Don't cry.*

"I wish we'd treated each other better." I said. "We should've been kinder and more patient. We fought too much and laughed too little. We missed so many opportunities."

Dwelling on regrets only makes things harder. Try to separate regret and guilt from genuine sadness. I know you feel lost and lonely, but some of that is self-pity. Besides, you're not alone--I'm with you all the time.

Waves rolled onto the rocky beach, dissolving into ripples of lacy white foam. Two scuba divers wearing wetsuits braced themselves against the ocean's slap and tug as they shuffled into the water, carrying heavy oxygen tanks on their backs. Half a mile out, a sailboat tacked toward Halibut Point State Park.

The difficulties we went through were necessary for our growth, Ron continued. *One thing we both learned was not to give up and run away when things got tough, which was our usual MO. Instead, we hung in there for thirteen years through good times and bad.*

"We'd finally come to understand how important that was, just before you left. Things between us were getting better."

We learned the value of loyalty, devotion, and perseverance. Still, we kept our walls in place. We didn't reveal our deepest feelings openly because we feared being vulnerable. We were scared of getting hurt. I pushed you away with my anger and you tried to hide your emotions from me. Now we're able to express ourselves without reservation. We couldn't have gotten to this stage in our relationship if I'd remained embodied. I love you more now than when I lived on earth, or at least I'm more aware of it and more open about it because the resistance and ego are gone. I'm more relaxed and more patient now--there's no longer any stress or conflict.

"Why couldn't we have handled things better while you were still here, instead of waiting until after you'd gone home to figure it out?" I lamented.

Don't worry, we have many more lifetimes to go. We'll do better next time.

I shifted my position on the rock, straightening a leg that had begun to cramp, and contemplated what he'd said. Fear and defensiveness had always stood in the way of our happiness. It was probably the same for a lot of people.

You've learned other valuable lessons, too, since I left earth. The greatest expression of love is letting go of those you love. You did what was right for me, even though it hurt you. Despite your pain, you honored my wishes, kept your promise to me, and showed dignity in the face of great suffering.

I heard the words of Sting's song "If You Love Somebody Set Them Free" playing inside my head.

I wish I hadn't been the one to put you through that, but you'd never loved anyone else enough to experience the intensity of what you needed to experience. And you wouldn't have been interested enough to pursue the truth about what happens after the body dies.

The wind ruffled my hair and I felt Ron stroking it back into place.

With me you learned to love deeply. Now you need to learn to love broadly. Take the love you feel for me and expand it to encompass everyone and everything. He suggested I read Sufi literature, especially the poems of Rumi and Hafiz, to understand more about elevating personal love to a spiritual level. *Okay, enough for now. It's time for lunch. Eat a lobster roll for me.*

I stood up and climbed over the rocks, down to the beach. When I reached the last boulder I spotted a pyramid-shaped pattern lined up carefully on its flat surface. Drawing closer I saw the purple shell of a sea urchin at the top, two sand dollars beneath it, and three scallop shells in the bottom row--and I knew Ron had placed them there for me. I scooped up the shells and slid them into my pocket.

• • •

The next morning, I awoke to the "sound" of Ron's voice. *I don't want you to keep holding onto regrets, bemoaning what should or shouldn't have been. That just makes you more unhappy.*

"I know," I admitted. "I'm trying . . ."

If you want to, you can change something that happened in the so-called past, he said.

"How is that possible?"

Because time is an illusion. There really isn't any such thing as past or future. Here's what you do. When you're meditating, think about a situation you want to change, maybe an argument we had or something unkind that one of us did. Hold the memory in your mind and feel what you felt at that time--really feel it. Then infuse the scenario with the pink light of love you experienced when you visited here, at home. Imagine a cloud of light surrounding everything. Let that light dissolve the anger, hurt, or discord in the situation and replace it with love. Create a mental picture of a better, more peaceful, more joyful interaction and let it replace the unhappy one.

"That's all I have to do? It sounds too simple."

I thought about the Norse goddess Frigg, whom mythology says weaves the web of fate. By reweaving portions of the web, she alters the course of human destiny.

We created the unwanted situation, we can un-create it and re-create another in its place, Ron explained. *Nothing's fixed. We're constantly creating our realities.*

A quote attributed to the Buddha popped into my mind: "With our thoughts we make the world."

"You put that in my head, didn't you?" I asked.

I just reminded you. He's right, you know. And here's another thing. If you rework past events, you'll save time when you get to your life review because you'll have already resolved the situation through the power of love.

• • •

My vacation ended few days later, and I flew back to Texas. Throughout the trip I sensed Ron guiding the planes--directing the human pilots and the air traffic controllers--and felt completely safe.

I can take much better care of you now than I could when I was in my old body, he told me. *I worried about you all the time when I was still there, because I didn't always know where you were or what you were doing and I couldn't control what happened to you.*

Two summers ago, I'd driven the 2,000-plus miles from our ranch in Texas to Massachusetts with my seventeen-year-old cat Domino. I'd planned to stay in Gloucester for two months and didn't want to leave her with a caretaker for that long. But I also wanted to challenge myself to see if I could overcome my fear of driving such a distance alone.

Ron was furious with me. He tried scaring me, pointing out all the possible pitfalls I might encounter along the way. He even offered to buy plane seats for both me *and* Domino. I stubbornly resisted, both for practical reasons--I'd need a car while I was away--and to assert my independence.

I was a nervous wreck the whole time you were on the road, he admitted.

Indeed, he'd phoned me half a dozen times a day, every day, to check where I was. As I cruised down the highways, I dutifully noted the towns I passed and the exit numbers, so I could report my location when he called. In September, when my vacation ended, he flew to Massachusetts and traveled back with me, insisting he couldn't bear to let me make the cross-country trip again alone. I was glad he did--not only because I enjoyed his company, but because the trip turned into a smorgasbord of natural disasters: a hurricane in Massachusetts, an earthquake in New York, a flood in Pennsylvania, and wildfires in East Texas.

Now I'm with you all the time, every step you take. I heard him singing the Police's song "Every Breath You Take" and felt gratitude for his vigilant protection.

CHAPTER 23

After my visit to the place Ron called "home," I began wondering if I could journey to other places beyond earth as well. When I asked him about it one morning in meditation he laughed, then showed me a picture of him slipping his feet into a pair of walking shoes.

Where would you like to go?

"Anyplace you think I should know about," I said.

Come with me.

Taking me by the hand, he led me to the edge of what, to me, seemed like the end of the world. From my vantage point, the sky blazed a brilliant magenta streaked with pale yellow, as if the sun were shining through rubies.

"What an amazing sunset," I said.

He tugged at my hand. *Move into the red light with me.*

Usually I considered red a hot and stimulating color, but the soothing, peaceful nature of this substanceless red realm surprised me. I felt serene and weightless, as if I were floating on a cloud. It reminded me of the beautiful pink light that had enveloped me when I first visited Ron's home, but calmer. Nearby, I sensed the presence of other beings, all silent and immobile.

Several years ago, I'd visited a spa in New Mexico, north of Santa Fe. After bathing in mineral springs, I'd been wrapped in a warm sheet by an attendant and laid on a narrow bed in a darkened chamber along with dozens of other people to rest. In some ways this place reminded me of that experience, except it was infinitely more pleasant.

"Where are we?" I asked.

This is a place for rest and renewal.

"What about the other beings here?" I couldn't see them, but I felt their presence as keenly as if they were physical.

They're sleeping.

"Is this what it's like for a baby in the womb?"

No. Here the purpose is to be quiet, to stop thinking. Babies think a lot and they're aware of all kinds of things. Being inutero isn't as peaceful as you might think. This is a place of transition, a stop-over. Souls come here to rest after their lifetimes on earth or elsewhere, before moving on to the next stage.

Before I'd finished formulating my next thought, Ron answered, *You can come here any time you feel a need for comfort and rejuvenation. You don't have to be "dead"--this place is available to everyone.*

A few days later, Ron shepherded me to another place he called the Aquamarine Chamber. As we slid into it, I felt as if I were underwater in a swimming pool, looking at the sun shining through the turquoise water. The aqua glow not only surrounded me, it swirled through me as well, cleansing me inside and out. After a few moments, my vision adjusted and I realized I was suspended within a multifaceted capsule. Light refracted differently through each facet.

"It's like being inside a crystal," I said.

When the glowing rays touched me, I felt a tingling sensation all over my body, as if I'd been submerged in a vat of champagne. I sensed gentle adjustments being made within my mind and body. With each subtle shift, a pleasant current of energy rippled up from my toes to my head.

This is a place of clearing and attunement, Ron explained. *The light dissolves all the psychic debris that accumulates during a lifetime on earth and realigns the fragments so that everything functions harmoniously again. The soul can be wounded by a painful or difficult lifetime. Souls are indestructible, but they're not invulnerable to injury and suffering. This is where souls come after shedding their physical bodies, so they can recuperate.*

Dr. Brian Weiss, in his book *Miracles Happen,* writes about people whose souls had reincarnated into bodies with ailments or impediments that were rooted in their previous lifetimes. One man developed cancer of the stomach, the place where he'd been shot and killed in another lifetime. A woman who had died in two prior incarnations from eating a particular spice came into this life with an allergy to that spice. A boy whose legs were crushed in an earlier incarnation walked with difficulty in his current body. In *You Cannot Die,* Dr. Ian Currie recounts the story of an Indian boy who was born with a strange birthmark on his neck; the mark mirrored the razor cut that had ended his former life.

That's a reason why many souls choose to go through healing treatments after coming home, before they return to earth again, Ron pointed out. *But you don't have to wait until you're done with your physical body to visit here. You can begin the process of healing while you're still living on earth. In fact, that's probably a good idea. Now that you know the way, you can come back whenever you feel the need.*

• • •

A week later, we visited a pretty, green realm that made me think of stripy malachite, except it appeared translucent rather than solid. Upon entering it, I felt its cool, slimy texture, as if seaweed were brushing my skin. When we journeyed deeper into the green world, its striations grew more distinct. Light and dark bands of color wound around each other, and within the bands I sensed the presence of minuscule, primitive life forms, perhaps a type of algae. Although I couldn't see them, I knew they saw me.

"Does this world exist?" I asked Ron.

Infinite worlds exist, but they're not "worlds" exactly, or places either, at least not in the usual sense. They're levels of light and resonance, he replied.

"Do all of them have specific purposes?"

I suppose so, but I don't really know. You interpret everything according to your own perception--the slimy seaweed, the crystalline capsule, and so on--but it's true meaning may be something else entirely that you can't comprehend. Or it may have no meaning at all--it just is. The same holds true on earth.

"How can I know what's real?" I asked, frustrated.

Everything is real and not-real.

"What about the places we go during dreams?"

One night I'd dreamed of entering a spacious white room where a woman dressed in white used music to weave gossamer cloth as soft as clouds. The cloth emerged in wispy strands from silver rods that hung from the ceiling. By varying the musical tones, she produced subtly different patterns and textures. The dream reminded me of the Greek Moirae or Fates, three sister deities who spun, wove, and cut the threads that formed human lives.

The dreamscape does exist, but it's not the same place as the home where I live now, nor is it like earth or the nonphysical worlds we've visited together. It's another level within the whole. You can read Australian Aborigine stories to find out more. You and I meet there sometimes.

Over the years, both before and after Ron passed from earth, I frequently dreamed of visiting a town in Wiltshire, England with him. In the dream, we stayed in a charming, antique house made of native stone with an attached greenhouse beside a stream. Despite the fact that it was always raining in my dream, I felt content and comfortable there. I assumed the dream and its familiar, pleasant ambiance had been inspired by the happy trip Ron and I had taken in December 2000 to Stonehenge and vicinity.

It has older roots, he pointed out. Several centuries ago, he explained, we'd lived in that house together and operated the tavern that adjoined it. *It was one of our few happy lifetimes.* He chuckled, then added, *Maybe that's why I enjoyed my bar life so much this last time around.*

An image of the Nine of Cups from the *Gilded Tarot* deck, a picture of a jovial barkeep raising a chalice, popped into my mind. "It's a past-life memory?" I asked. "Is the house still there?"

No, not physically. But it still exists in your consciousness--it's not just a memory. Nothing that's ever existed is ever gone. That's why we can go back there, although your interpretation is a contemporary one. I'm showing you these places to help you understand that Skye Alexander living on earth in the twenty-first century is only one tiny sliver of stained glass in a magnificent rose window.

In 2020, while shopping in a secondhand store, I stumbled upon a watercolor painting of an old stone house beside a stream. It looked remarkably like the place I remembered. Now it hangs in my art studio and makes me happy whenever I look at it.

• • •

Sometime after my sojourns to the ruby-colored world and the Aquamarine Chamber, I listened to a medium named Susanne Wilson speak about what she called "halls of healing" where she said souls go to rest after incarnating on earth. I read something in Michael Newton's book *Destiny of Souls* that also validated my experiences. According to Newton, "Quite a number of my subjects have told me that between their lives on Earth they travel as discarnates to other worlds both in and out of our dimension. Some explain that they see other nonphysical entities on these trips."

His clients, while under hypnosis, also described something similar to the Aquamarine Chamber I'd witnessed. Just as Ron told me, they said that souls could be damaged while living on earth and, after leaving their host bodies, the souls sought periods of healing and reorientation. Most souls required some attunement. Many of them go to something called a "crystalline enclosure." As one of Newton's subjects recounted, "My place of recovery is crystalline in composition . . . The crystal walls have multicolored stones which reflect prisms of light. The geometric angles of these crystals send out moving bands of light which crisscross around and bring clarity to my thoughts."

The idea that souls could benefit from being in the presence of crystals--even nonphysical ones--made perfect sense to me. Since ancient times, people have used gemstones for healing purposes. Birthstones, for instance, were initially worn to strengthen a person's innate weaknesses or moderate extremes in character. Human healers who work with crystals and gemstones talk about the stones' powers to facilitate alignment and to balance the flow of energy in the physical body. "Their crystalline structure can absorb, conserve, focus, and emit energy," writes Judy Hall in *The Encyclopedia of Crystals.*

Colored light also contains healing properties. The practice of using color for therapeutic purposes, what's known as chromatherapy, draws upon the frequencies of different hues to alleviate physical, emotional, and mental conditions.

Our ancestors knew about this too. The stained-glass windows of Europe's great cathedrals weren't designed solely for aesthetics, they could also influence health and well-being. In *Sacred Architecture,* A.T. Mann writes "it was believed that the light passing through the windows was transformed or transmuted and therefore had a healing and revivifying effect upon the people gathered within the cathedral."

Holistic healers frequently speak of resonance. Many therapeutic practices including acupuncture, homeopathy, and Reiki work with the body's energy patterns to adjust imbalances and restore harmonious resonance throughout a patient's system. The most powerful resonance of all is the frequency of love. I thought about the pink light Ron showed me in his home, how it enveloped that realm in a web of joy.

The energy of love holds everything together, he'd explained, *the way the ocean holds all the sea creatures together, except it's weightless and doesn't impede movement. That love resonance exists on earth too, but you're not always aware of it--people are usually attuned to the vibration of fear instead. The more you can align yourself with the frequency of love, the happier and healthier you'll be.*

CHAPTER 24

During my morning walk on the ranch, Ron asked, *Do you remember when I showed you the light in your heart chakra?*

While he was still in his physical body we walked together often, although I didn't know until after he'd gone home just how much pain that caused him. In his teens, he'd broken his back and his right hip playing football, but in those days the treatment options we have today didn't exist. He'd healed badly and suffered for nearly five decades until he'd finally had both hips replaced. Years of basketball, running, skiing, tennis, and other sports--plus parachute jumping when he was in the Air Force--had taken their toll as well, damaging his knees and feet.

I never took a step without pain. Now everything's easy. You can't imagine how glad I am to be rid of that old body.

Before I saw a car barrel around a curve, I felt Ron nudge me off the pavement and into the grass. *Get off the road,* he ordered.

"Thanks, darlin'," I said as the car whizzed by. "What were you saying about the light in my heart chakra?"

Remember I told you that it's a piece of home--the place where I am now--and that you brought it with you when you came to earth? The light of love, your "love light."

"Yes."

Since he'd first put me in touch with the light that glowed within my torso and showed me how to perceive the enlivening energy in the roses at my friend Claire's home in Massachusetts, I'd been trying to increase my awareness. The idea that the light-energy connected me to Ron, to beings on the other side, and to everything in the universe was reassuring.

It's sometimes thought of--inadequately--as vitality or enthusiasm or passion. It keeps the body alive. A good analogy might be a battery, a power source you carry with you when you incarnate.

"We need a generator to support us while we're on Planet Earth?" I asked.

I sensed him nodding. *It's hard putting these things into words, language is too limited. Anyway, the demands we deal with on earth can quickly burn out the physical body and it needs constant recharging. When the power wanes, you get sick. You have a connection between here and there, through which you can download energy. You could think of it as a cosmic electric cord that connects to your body. Light from home flows through it, rejuvenating you, usually at night while you sleep.*

I thought about the healing modality known as Reiki, a word that translates as "guided life force energy." My friend Anne, a Reiki master and teacher, calls it the energy of love. According to some Indian philosophies, life energy or "prana" enters the body through centers known as chakras. Stress, sorrow, and emotional upsets can drain our vitality and manifest in physical ailments. Dis-ease, as holistic healers might suggest, leads to disease. Was love the antidote to every health problem? That's what Ron seemed to be saying.

Your job is to shine this light of love into the world, he continued. *Not only you, everyone is given that task, but most people let fear block the light. That's what I did--I wasn't open to receive the energy flowing toward me anymore, I wasn't getting enough juice. I had to come back home to renew myself.*

I sensed him sigh. Did he have regrets too?

Everything is light, made up of light, enlivened by light, propelled by light. On earth, you tend to emphasize substance, but that's an illusion--without light, substance can't exist. Don't hide your light, baby. Whenever you feel scared or discouraged or lonely, focus on the light in you and envision it expanding until it encompasses everyone and everything.

"That's a pretty tall order."

It is. Okay, here's something easy you can do--I think the Dalai Lama may have recommended it. When you breathe in, cherish yourself. When you breathe out, cherish the world. Don't worry about doing it perfectly--you might feel silly at first or resistant, or you might feel nothing at all. Just keep at it.

Recalling Ron's negative attitudes about spirituality and religion while he was embodied, I had trouble reconciling what he told me now with the ideas the man I'd known had held. He certainly wouldn't have sought advice from the Dalai Lama or read Rumi's poetry. Suddenly, I heard him singing an old song, "This Little Light of Mine," that I remembered from Sunday school in my childhood, and I laughed at the incongruity.

You've heard that when souls leave their physical bodies they pass through a tunnel that leads to a brilliant white light, right?

"Yes," I answered.

When they're drawn to that beam of light, they're homing in on the loving energy that animates all life. You can't imagine what a rush it is! That's why people who've had near-death experiences talk about feeling an incredible sense of joy, peace, and safety when they encounter the light. A bit of that light is always within you and you can access it whenever you like.

"You keep telling me that."

I keep telling you because it's important. Sorry if I sound like I'm browbeating you, but it's the truth. Every moment you have a choice. Every moment you can perpetuate fear or you can shine light into the world. You can focus on loss and unhappiness, or you can be grateful for the good things in your life. You can feel sorry for yourself or you can try to make things better for everyone on earth, including yourself. You don't need to do anything grand. Small acts of kindness count too, like helping an old person in the supermarket reach something on the bottom shelf. Those seemingly inconsequential acts add up--you'll see when you get to your life review.

I'd heard the term "lightworkers," which refers to people who bring healing, peace, and love to earth. According to author Doreen Virtue, these individuals "volunteered, before birth, to help the planet and its population heal from the effects of fear." It seemed Ron was guiding me in that direction. Had I, too, volunteered for this task before coming to earth?

Wear the ring I gave you, he said. *It can help.*

His words surprised me. Years ago Ron suggested getting his deceased mother's diamond engagement ring reset for me. At the time I'd been confused, uncertain what the overture meant to him, and I hadn't shown much enthusiasm. The ring still sat in a safe deposit box in the bank. Was he suggesting the ring could help me?

When I finally did slip the ring on my finger I understood instantly. The brilliant diamond sparkled as if illuminated by an inner light, while also seeming to increase the ambient light it reflected. It changed colors too. Sometimes it shone a pure, radiant white, sometimes pale blue, and sometimes a delicate pink.

I realized this gift of love offered me a beautiful connection to my own light and the animating force of the universe.

• • •

On the morning of the autumn equinox, Ron asked if I'd like to go on a journey. I jumped at the chance. A couple weeks had passed since we'd traveled together to the ruby-red world and the Aquamarine Chamber, and I was eager to explore more of the universe. I sat in the big, comfy chair in my bedroom and eased into a trance state. After a few minutes, my consciousness lifted out of my body, through the top of my head, and soared high above the earth.

From this elevated vantage point I saw a dazzling white light circling the planet, not at the equator but around the poles. It appeared to be a ring of crystalline mountains that sparkled with an amazingly brilliant light. They reminded me of the many points of the apophyllite that sits on a windowsill in my house. People who work with crystals prize apophyllites for their ability to amplify the amount of sunlight shining on them. The crystal mountains I observed below were not only magnitudes larger, but infinitely brighter as well.

The light isn't caused by the sun glinting off the mountains, Ron explained. *It's generated by the entities that live inside. These mountains and their inhabitants channel energy, knowledge, and awareness to beings on earth,* he continued. *They capture light and information from the cosmos and project it around the globe. Of course, none of this is physical. Even some places in our universe that seem dark to humans actually resonate with a great deal of energetic light--it's just not visible to the physical eye.*

The mysterious continent of Atlantis came to mind as I gazed in awe at the crystalline mountain range, which ran longitudinally through the middle of the Atlantic Ocean--right where myths say Atlantis was located. Legends tell us powerful crystals abounded on Atlantis, and powerful crystal workers lived there too. Atlanteans who knew how to use the stones supposedly accomplished great feats. Their desire for power, however, may have led to the destruction of the mythic land that continues to baffle researchers. Did it ever actually exist in the material world, or was it merely an allegorical place as Plato postulated?

My thoughts shifted to the place Ron called home and the indescribable light I'd witnessed during my visit there. Again, I recalled the accounts of people who've had near-death experiences and the radiant light they spoke about on the other side. Light, love, and life seemed to be inseparable, interwoven like a wondrous tapestry.

According to the creation story in Genesis, God's first command was "Let there be light." Might "light" in this case have referred not to daylight and sunshine, but to consciousness and love?

CHAPTER 25

Volcanoes erupted in record numbers during 2013--eighty-three by December, instead of the usual fifty to sixty per year. Months ago, Ron had discussed some exciting environmental work he'd been engaged in lately. Among other things, it involved dealing with volcanoes and their impact.

I'm part of a team that tries to mitigate chaos resulting from natural disasters, and to ease the suffering that results during such crises.

He'd seemed animated and enthusiastic, eager to share his experiences with me. Apparently, this new endeavor held more appeal for him than guiding airplanes through the skies or protecting me and his other friends. Ron had always loved weather and geography. His career as an air traffic controller had honed his meteorological skills, and his extensive travels throughout the world taught him geography firsthand.

As if responding to my thoughts, he punned, *I was bored to death on earth. I'd finished what I came to do and I had nothing more to contribute. It was time to move on. I can be of more use doing what I'm doing now. I can learn more too. After we leave our physical bodies, souls keep learning and growing through challenges, just as we do on earth. We can try our*

*hands at pretty much anything that piques our curiosity.
It's a continual process of awakening and expanding.*

"What exactly do you do with the earthquakes and volcanoes?" I asked.

Jocelyn might be able to design pretty flowers, and I could imagine spirits feeding information to humans in order to lead them toward worthwhile discoveries. But manipulating the course of natural disasters seemed far more complex and difficult. The way he explained it, though, made the process sound simple.

It's pretty straightforward, really. Spirits burrow into the earth and try to ease tension there, before a crisis happens--like a masseur relaxing tight muscles so they don't pull bones out of alignment. If we find a break somewhere in the earth's crust we reposition the tectonic plates--the way a doctor might realign sections of a broken bone--and then stick on some psychic Duct Tape to hold the pieces in place. Problem fixed.

Polynesian and Hawaiian myths tell stories about a tempestuous volcano goddess named Pele, who was said to wreak fiery devastation during her violent rages. People tried to protect themselves from her rampages with rituals and offerings. Supposedly, after seeing the destruction caused by her tantrums, Pele felt remorse and made amends by creating something of beauty.

Ron had lived in Hawaii for nearly twenty years, so I couldn't help asking, "Do you have to appease Pele with gifts?"

I heard him chuckle. *I wouldn't want to have a run-in with her! The scientific explanation for the increased volcanic activity is climate change. What scientists don't understand, though, is that the psychic and emotional stresses humans foist on the planet cause disruptions too. So much disharmony exists in your world and it impacts nature. Remember, everything's connected. The earth reacts to the energy of anger, hate, fear, and violence by producing what you call "natural disasters."*

I asked him to explain further and he gave me an analogy. *When you put excessive stress on a bridge or a building, it's likely to snap under the pressure. The same holds true for human beings--their bodies respond to stress with heart attacks, strokes, and so on. Earth can only cope with a certain amount of stress, too, before it breaks. The planet is a living entity, you know. Conflict causes fissions within earth's body. Anger erupts in volcanoes. Confusion manifests as tornadoes. Look in a mirror if you want to see the source of your problems. In some ways, the ancients may have had a better understanding of natural disasters than people do today.*

I considered the many ways healers of various stripes were trying to care for the earth: organic farmers, labyrinth wrights, monks chanting prayers for peace, crystal workers configuring energy grids, and on and on. Could their combined efforts offset the destructive forces operating on our planet? Would the voice of peace win out over the voice of fear? I hoped so.

• • •

In his book *Only Love Is Real,* Dr. Brian Weiss uses the analogy of a tree to describe our interconnectedness with everyone else. The people closest to you--family, lovers, friends--are like leaves on the same twig. Those in your wider circle, including colleagues and casual acquaintances, can be compared to the leaves on other twigs on the same branch. The leaves on other branches--your community, state, country, etc.--are all part of the same tree and all connected to you. When viewed in this way, spiritual teachings such as Jesus' words "Whatever you do to the least of my brothers and sisters you do to me" make literal sense.

The more Ron and I communicated, the more I understood about the connections between everything in the universe. Having studied astrology for many years, I knew how powerfully the heavenly bodies affect not only human beings, but societies, weather patterns, and earth changes as well. Our ancestors were attuned to cosmic influences, even if they lacked modern sophisticated science to confirm what they knew.

I was beginning to see the synergy of nonphysical and physical entities, of ethereal worlds and material ones. We're all part of the same continuum, which in reality has no past or future, only the infinite present.

• • •

The concept of an absence of time, no past, present, or future, is hardly new. More than thirty years ago, Dr. Raymond Moody wrote in his book *Reflections on Life*

After Life, "Several people have told me that during their encounters with 'death,' they got glimpses of an entirely separate realm of existence in which all knowledge--whether of past, present, or future-- seemed to co-exist in a sort of timeless state." Dr. Brian Weiss, in his book *Only Love Is Real,* proposes that our experience of time is a byproduct of the spirit tamping itself down to a slower vibration when it enters the dense, physical state.

Buddhist philosophy recommends that we let go of our perceptions of time as linear--the *Bhaddekaratta Sutta* instructs us not to "chase after the past or place expectations on the future." In his book *The Power of Now* Eckhart Tolle writes that now "is the *only* thing. It's all there is. The eternal present is the space within which your whole life unfolds."

While I was still grappling with the idea, Ron hit me with yet another revelation, one that taxed my conception of existence even further.

Everything has already been decided, he told me. *You don't have to worry about anything because it's all taken care of.*

I'd taken advantage of this relatively cool, cloudy fall day to do some yard work: digging bone meal into the soil around my irises, trimming dead sections from my rosemary bush, and planting tulip bulbs that I hoped would bloom in the spring. I stood up, stretched, and asked, "What do you mean?"

What you think of as your life now is really only a memory. It's already happened, just like all your other so-called "past" lives have already happened. In the same way you re-experience previous incarnations you're re-experiencing this one, but from a different perspective. The earth doesn't exist anymore either-- that's an illusion. It's a memory too. You think you're living on earth now, as Skye, but you're actually someplace else, many someplace elses, you just don't realize that yet. The dreams you have of yourself when you're asleep are no more real or unreal than the dreams you have about yourself when you're awake.

Vaguely I recalled having read something similar years ago in *A Course in Miracles.* "Is that because there's no delineation between past, present, and future?"

Think of it as a book. The whole story has been told and it's all written down right there in the book. Some of us are at the beginning of the story, some in the middle, and some near the end. As you approach the end, you understand more about what's happening than you did in Chapter 1. Regardless of what part you're reading at the moment, however, the end has already been written.

Trying to digest what he'd said, I asked, "What if the author decides to rewrite the book, like *The Magus?*" John Fowles' postmodern novel, which both Ron and I liked, had originally been published in 1965. Twelve years later, Fowles brought out a revised edition.

He laughed, but didn't answer. Instead he sang the nursery rhyme: "Row, row, row your boat gently down the stream. Merrily, merrily, merrily, merrily, life is but a dream."

CHAPTER 26

"What else do you do when you're not busy disarming volcanoes and saving the world from destruction?" I asked Ron.

As I gazed at a framed photo of him that sat on my dresser, I thought I saw a wisp of his beautiful white hair lift slightly, as if blown by a gentle breeze. Were my eyes playing tricks on me? Or had he chosen this method to get my attention? In the coming weeks, I would witness the same visual peculiarity several times in connection with different photographs. Despite the recurring phenomena, I couldn't explain it.

In response to my question, Ron said, *I play football with my brother and some other guys.*

His reply surprised me. Playing football in heaven? Ron had always loved football--the closest he came to finding happiness on earth was on the gridiron. Ron was, after all, a warrior soul and football is a war game. He'd starred as the quarterback on his high school team, and then played semi-pro when he was in his twenties. Despite his speed, savvy, and a general's keen sense of battle strategy, he'd lacked the height and weight to achieve his dream of making it to the NFL.

We don't just sit around on clouds playing harps, you know, he teased. *It's not all work either--we have fun here too.*

I struggled to imagine orbs of colored light tossing a football around a celestial playing field. I didn't even understand the rules of football in America, never mind in the afterlife.

"How does that work?"

I heard him laughing. *Admittedly, it's a little tricky. We do everything mentally. We use our thoughts to move the ball around the field. We block our opponents mentally too--no tackling or body checking, considering we don't have physical bodies here. The hardest part is we can all read each other's minds, so we know what everyone else is thinking.*

"No huddles? No secret signals?"

We shroud our thoughts by generating a smokescreen of mental activity around our plays. We bombard our opponents with a whole slew of images simultaneously, to create confusion. It's a great tactic, very challenging, and difficult to pull off. Teamwork on a high level.

I sensed he was enjoying this clever method of diversion even more than he'd enjoyed the strategy of earthly games. Remembering his discussion of working through the minds of human air traffic controllers and other people on earth, feeding them information, I couldn't help wondering if sports-loving spirits also intervened in athletic events.

Before I could ask, he replied. *Sometimes you see moves on the field that seem impossible and you think nobody could do that. Even the guy who made the play can't believe it happened and couldn't explain how he accomplished such a feat. In some of those instances-- not all, though--a being on this side had a hand in it. A strong, well-focused thought can push the football just inside the goal post. A quick heads-up can put a wide receiver in exactly the right place to catch a pass.*

If spirits could tamper with computers and electric lights and make rose quartz crystals appear out of nowhere, surely they could nudge a ball a few inches one way or the other.

"Doesn't that mess with the betting odds?" I asked.

Of course, he answered. *That's part of the fun.*

• • •

Revelations may come to us when we're deep in meditation or kneeling in a church sanctuary, but they also present themselves while we're engaged in the most mundane daily tasks. When we're performing apparently insignificant chores, our minds are relaxed and receptive to communication from our inner selves as well as from beings elsewhere in the cosmos. This afternoon, while I folded laundry, I found myself wondering about Ron's lifetimes as a warrior and a leader. The thoughts had barely formed in my mind when I sensed his presence and heard him respond.

When humans leave their bodies, they don't turn into angels. Our basic natures don't really change much

203

after we leave our host bodies. Serious souls remain serious, pranksters continue playing jokes.

"Tell me more about it--help me understand," I said.

I had many lifetimes as a leader and a warrior. That's why I always took charge in this one--on the playing field, as an air traffic controller. Even in barroom brawls I was the one in command.

He'd told me about some of the fights he'd gotten into and I remembered the wild stories his old friends had shared with me after he passed.

I enjoyed the role, he continued. *It probably hampered me when it came to relating to people in other ways, though. I had a very sensitive side in my lifetime as Ron, but I tried not to show it--I didn't even want to acknowledge it myself because empathy is a liability for a warrior. In the future I may choose lifetimes where I'll learn to handle situations in other ways.*

"If everything is already decided, don't you already know about all those so-called future lifetimes?" I asked as I stacked a week's worth of underwear in the top drawer of my dresser.

To some extent. It's not as clear as you might imagine. Even here many things are shielded from us.

"Maybe you'll come back as a woman next time," I said and heard him chuckle.

Until Ron began talking to me from the afterlife, I believed souls had to reincarnate into every possible situation and station in life--pauper, ruler, farmer, criminal, teacher, doctor--in order to experience the fullness of earthly existence and to grow into well-rounded beings. As I understood him, however, that's not the case.

For the most part, we choose lifetimes that fall more or less within the scope of our soul roles. We pick the ones that will be most useful to us, that utilize our proclivities, as well as those from which we can learn things we want to learn. The decision is always up to the individual soul, although our teachers and guides help us determine what's best for us at any given time.

I stacked bath towels, still warm from the dryer, in the closet, then asked, "You mean I probably won't come back as a mountain climber or a fighter pilot?"

Unlikely. You can learn assertiveness or daring in ways that are better suited to your fundamental nature. You're never forced to take on a lifetime you don't want, even if it might serve you in some way. You can even avoid coming to earth completely, like your guides Megan and Moriah.

That sounded like a good idea to me--I had little interest in coming back to earth again if I didn't have to. I'd never felt I belonged on this planet anyway. I never seemed to completely inhabit my physical body. Usually it seemed as though I were floating slightly outside the boundaries of my physical form, observing it like an etymologist studying a bug.

As he often did, Ron read my mind and responded before I'd finished my thought. *You'd be further along if you'd accepted more lifetimes on earth. You shied away from hardships that would've helped you grow.*

According to what I'd witnessed I was a yellow soul, near the bottom of the otherworld's hierarchy. Ron had advanced to a rank above me, the level of gold. Although my childhood was difficult, most of my adult life had been pretty easy. I couldn't imagine suffering the horrible existences some people endured, even if doing so would propel me forward.

I picked up a bit of blue during my last go 'round, Ron interrupted. *I got some extra points for my part in 9/11.*

"Does this mean that unless I get busy you're going to move so far ahead of me I'll never see you again?"

Of course not--that's not even possible. You're part of my inner circle, which means we'll always be connected.

Recalling that he'd said he belonged to an extended group of about a hundred souls, I asked, "What about the others in your group?"

We'll stay connected too, though in a less direct way. We might have casual contact or we might live on the planet at the same time but never run into each other. Like air traffic controllers talking to pilots they never meet face-to-face. We're united in our purpose and the work we do. Even if we don't realize it, we influence one another. You have an impact on all those people who read your books, but you'll never know about it.

I thought again about the tree analogy Dr. Brian Weiss discussed in his book *Only Love Is Real.* He'd used it to describe connections between human beings, but it could just as easily symbolize relationships between souls: leaves on the same twig as souls in one's inner circle, those on other branches as the larger group.

Don't worry, Ron continued. *You won't get left behind. All souls continue evolving, and as they do they contribute to the evolution of their entire group.*

A cosmic team effort, I thought. "Am I making any progress this time around? Sometimes I feel like a hamster in a treadmill, running as fast as I can, yet going nowhere."

Sure, you always make progress. Even if you do a lot of things most people might consider futile or bad, your soul learns from those experiences. And you have an infinite number of chances to get it right. In life review, you come to understand how you could have managed better and you set new tasks for yourself, to further the growth process. If you got rich swindling people in one lifetime, for example, you might choose a lifetime in which you have to work hard just to get by or you might opt to be a philanthropist. It's not "an eye for an eye" though. The goal is to bring about balance.

Would I have to balance the comfortable, middle-class life I'd led this time around with one of poverty in the future? Would the freedom I now enjoyed be offset by an incarnation of infirmity or imprisonment? This might be the cushiest life I've ever had or ever will.

Make the best of it, Ron urged. *To ease your mind, you probably won't regress to a primitive lifetime after making it this far. You've lived hand-to-mouth existences before. You've been a slave, a prisoner, and an invalid. You gleaned what you needed from those experiences. In other lifetimes you'll seek out situations that test skills you haven't developed yet. Now you're learning independence, which was lacking in your previous incarnations. In the so-called past, few people, especially women, had much independence. In the future you may choose to wield more authority or learn to handle money effectively. Of course, it's all up to you. You get to pick the lives you want, starting right this minute.*

I remembered what he'd said before, that at every moment we have the choice to act from love or fear. With each thought, word, and deed we create not only the conditions of this existence, but future ones as well. His words reminded me of a Cherokee story about two wolves that an elder tells to his grandson. The wolves, named Love and Fear, live inside each of us and they fight all the time.

"Which wolf wins?" the boy asks. His grandfather answers, "The one you feed."

Actually, you're doing fine, Ron encouraged me. *You're among the youngest and lowest-ranking members of your soul group--they're mostly gold and blue souls. But you're working hard to get ahead, to learn as much as you can, as fast as you can, although for the record there's no "deadline."* He laughed at his pun.

His description reminded me of my early schooling. I'd skipped kindergarten and started first grade a year ahead of my peers, so I was always the youngest kid in class. In college I pursued two majors simultaneously, carrying a heavier workload each term than my fellow students, while also working part-time. Even so, I'd excelled and graduated with honors.

"How do we know when we're doing what we're supposed to be doing?" I asked.

Usually you don't--that's part of the challenge. If you knew ahead of time exactly what you were supposed to do, it would be too easy. When you feel joyful and things seem to fall into place seamlessly, you're most likely on the right track. Here's another thing: Pay attention to so-called coincidences. Often those are prompts from us over here.

• • •

In the days that followed, I began seeing the number 11 pop up with increased regularity. I just "happened" to glance at the clock at 9:11, 11:11, 1:11, and so on. An important email might come through at 3:11. A sales receipt might show a charge of $16.11, a book might fall open to page 11, or I'd spot a license plate with the number 11 on it.

Whenever this occurred I paused, observed, and listened. What had I been thinking, feeling, or doing at that moment? Frequently those thoughts, emotions, or actions turned out to be significant.

In the movie *I Origins,* a biologist has this same experience. It leads him to confront his beliefs, both scientific and spiritual, including those related to reincarnation and the afterlife. Some theories propose that when you see 11:11, a portal is opening, perhaps to another level of consciousness. Others suggest this moment offers expanded opportunities or insights.

For me, 11 has both astrological and numerological significance. Its appearance also meant Ron was trying to get my attention. One morning at exactly 11:11 he reminded me, *Eleven is the number of souls in your inner circle.*

Who were they, I wondered? Ron, of course, and maybe Lyndsey--but who else? Who among them were currently living on earth? I thought about my friends Leslie (who'd introduced me to Ron), Claire, and Anne. My sister Myke to whom I'd always been close. What about people who'd passed through my life only briefly, yet impacted me profoundly?

A week or so later I began seeing hearts in nature. Heart-shaped rocks. Leaves shaped like hearts. Prickly pear cacti with heart-shaped paddles. Yet another reminder, I realized.

The heart is the center of wisdom, not the brain, Ron explained. *The brain holds facts and figures, but the heart holds truth. It's no accident that the heart is at the center of the body. It's no accident that the heart sustains life by pumping blood through the body. And it's no accident that we associate the heart with love, because love is the source and sustenance of life, on earth and elsewhere. Whenever you doubt or feel anxious, look to your heart and it will guide you.*

While he was embodied, Ron never spoke about such things. Even after all these months, some of the ideas he expressed--which he would have considered woo-woo or unscientific or silly before--surprised me. I could only listen in awe as he shared his expanded vision and guidance with me, and feel grateful.

CHAPTER 27

During meditation one October morning, Ron asked, *Remember how I used to joke that one day we could vacation on Mars? Come on, I'll show you what it's like there.*

I relaxed into a deeper level of trance and felt myself being drawn up through the top of my head, high into the sky above, until I could no longer see anything I recognized on earth. I floated around for a bit before slowly descending to a place where the colors were all wrong. A red sky hung above yellow mountains. Patches of blackened fields, reminiscent of the charred land in East Texas after the wildfires of 2011, stretched beneath me.

Ron led me by the hand, the way he used to do when we crossed busy streets on earth, down a winding road that glowed brilliant gold and into which our feet disappeared. The phrase "streets paved with gold" flashed in my mind, although I knew we weren't in heaven.

After a while, we came to a town where adobe-like buildings with flat roofs stood on both sides of the golden road. The structures resembled houses I'd seen in Santa Fe. As I drew closer I realized they weren't solid; they were made of light. Throngs of white orbs filled the scene, like the ones that populated the realm Ron showed me on our first extraterrestrial journey together to the place he called home.

"Where are we?" I asked.

Mars.

"Why are all those white orbs here?"

Souls evolve in many places. We experience different things on Mars than we can on earth. Young souls come here to learn basic survival skills and to gain awareness of themselves as individuals. They're not human, of course, but they're similar to young souls incarnating on earth, who live in primitive conditions where they endure constant hardships. After they mature, which may take millennia, they can devote themselves to intellectual pursuits and other tasks.

"Will they come to earth then?"

Possibly. He pointed to a silvery waterfall tumbling down from a rocky ridge. *Look.*

"I didn't know Mars had water on it."

At that time, 2013, scientists suspected Mars had ice caps and frozen lakes. But it didn't seem possible that running water would be present on a planet where surface temperatures could exceed minus 100 degrees Fahrenheit.

Soon they'll reveal that flowing water does, indeed, exist on Mars, Ron told me.

Two years later, on September 28, 2015, NASA posted a press release on its website describing the findings of the Mars Reconnaissance Orbiter. It said,

"Using an imaging spectrometer on MRO, researchers detected signatures of hydrated minerals on slopes where mysterious streaks are seen on the Red Planet. These darkish streaks appear to ebb and flow over time. They darken and appear to flow down steep slopes during warm seasons, and then fade in cooler seasons. They appear in several locations on Mars when temperatures are above minus 10 degrees Fahrenheit (minus 23 Celsius), and disappear at colder times . . . This is a significant development, as it appears to confirm that water--albeit briny--is flowing today on the surface of Mars."

• • •

I'd assumed that lifetimes on earth were mandatory, like attending grades K-12, but a better comparison is college where you can select from a variety of subjects and classes: earth, Mars, Sirius, the Pleiades, etc. A few weeks after our visit to Mars, Ron took me to Titan.

"Why are we were going there?" I asked.

He replied, *Why not?*

The only thing I knew about Titan was that it was one of Saturn's moons. I thought it would be more fun to skate around on Saturn's rings or bask in Venus's loving warmth. But if Ron wanted to show me Titan, I was ready to go. As I'd done so many times before, I slipped into a light trance, eased my consciousness out of my physical body, and let Ron guide me mentally through the solar system.

215

It's bright blue when you first approach it, but becomes darker blue when you move into it, he explained.

Soon I saw a blue sphere glowing against the black backdrop of space. As we slid into it, the sphere grew darker, denser, and icy cold. The color and pressure reminded me of being deep underwater. I sensed both actual water and a resonance I associated with water. It felt as if we floated in a small boat, bobbing about on big waves.

It can be a bit overwhelming, even scary, he warned. *Don't worry, we're okay.*

As I began to relax, I noticed glowing green ripples running through the inky water. They reminded me of the phosphorescence I'd seen along the shores of Cape Ann.

"What's that?" I asked.

The entities that live here. They're very primitive.

"What's their purpose?"

I don't know. Maybe they don't have a purpose, they just are.

When we'd seen enough, Ron took me by the hand and led me back to earth and into my physical body again. Before he left to go back to his home, he kissed me and said, *Write it down before you forget it.*

What was my purpose in witnessing this? Maybe to broaden my perception of the cosmos. Maybe to trust my experiences, to believe that the things I sensed and intuited--no matter how bizarre--had validity. By opening the doors of my perception, as William Blake had proposed, all things would become clear.

After I'd collected myself, I looked up Titan online and learned that it's composed primarily of water, ice mainly, and liquid methane lakes. Scientists believe it's the only body in our solar system, other than earth, with stable bodies of water. It also has a dense atmosphere twice as thick as earth's.

According to www.space.com: "There is also data that suggests the presence of a liquid ocean beneath the surface." Just as I'd experienced it! The photos on the site looked very much like what I witnessed too, except for an orangish section I hadn't noticed. The website's description read, "Global mosaic of Visual and Infrared Mapping Spectrometer (VIMS) images acquired during the nominal and equinox Cassini mission."

Almost four years later, on July 27, 2017, the website phys.org reported that according to "a new study published in *Astrophysical Journal Letters*, scientists identified some of the negatively charged species as what are known as 'carbon chain anions'." I didn't understand what that meant, but what followed rang true. "These linear molecules are understood to be building blocks towards more complex molecules, and may have acted as the basis for the earliest forms of life on Earth."

More evidence of our interconnectedness with all beings, all life, everywhere in the universe! Although the Cassini's plasma spectrometer hadn't captured the phosphorescence I'd seen, I believed it had detected the primitive entities I'd sensed during my sojourn to Titan.

• • •

Want to go to the Pleiades? Ron asked on another morning.

"Sure," I answered.

I rinsed my coffee mug and put it in the dishwasher, then relaxed into my comfy meditation chair. I'd intentionally avoided researching any of the heavenly bodies so I could visit them with an open mind, free of preconceptions that might influence my experience.

As we approached, Ron told me the cluster known as the "Seven Sisters" had formed from the explosion of a single star. Seven, I knew, was considered a sacred, magical number--there are seven colors in the visible spectrum, seven notes in a musical scale, seven major chakras in the human body, seven planets that we can see with the naked eye, seven days in a week.

They're all pieces of one star.

"That must be why they're called sisters, because they're all related."

The name comes from ancient Greek mythology, but the Egyptians and many other people knew about them too.

To me the stars looked like incredibly brilliant blue-white diamonds scattered on a black velvet cloth. As we neared the archipelago, however, I noticed the stars were actually different colors, albeit very pale. More surprising, each resonated with a particular musical note. I wondered if this was what the "music of the spheres" meant--except they weren't spheres. Instead, they appeared jagged and kind of spiky. Some even seemed to have holes in them that made me think of open mouths.

They're moving apart, very slowly, Ron explained. *Let's get a closer look. Which one do you want to check out?*

I indicated one that glowed with a hint of orange. The color wasn't consistent--part was yellowish and a faint olive-green band wound around it.

Listen to its sound.

"Hmm. It's D, I think, but I could be wrong. My musical education is limited."

As we drifted closer, I felt a tingling sensation and realized the star's resonance caused it. "Do souls come here to live?"

Souls can live pretty much anyplace they want to. Most souls who incarnate on earth visit the Pleiades at some time to gain wisdom and training that can help them get along as humans. Think you'd like to take up residence here?

"I guess I'd have to learn some more about the Pleiades first. What do souls learn here that can help them while they're on earth?"

How to heal with sound, for one thing. Everything's made of energy, you know, and energy vibrates. By

*attuning inharmonious energies you can heal body,
mind, and spirit.*

Sound healers, I knew, used singing bowls, tuning
forks, and other instruments to realign discordant
energies in body and mind, and to restore balance.
Hindus suggest that the sound "Om" is the sound of
creation. The term *Nada Brahma* translates as "all is
sound." Chanting, singing, and playing music can
produce ecstatic states and facilitate insight. I thought
about the saying "music soothes the savage beast," the
"beast" being our inner darkness.

*On the Pleiades souls also learn to amplify light.
They can draw on the stars' light and their memories of
living here to increase their own light when earth's
shadows block it.*

I remembered the diamond ring Ron had given me,
how it seemed to sparkle with inner light. He'd said it
would help me connect with my own light and that of
the universe. Although lately I'd forgotten to wear it, I
promised myself I would put it on as soon as I returned
from this journey. I also made a mental note to unpack
a crystal singing bowl I'd bought years ago and start
playing it again.

When we got back to earth, I slipped the ring on my
finger, then brought up the website earthsky.org on my
computer to learn more about the Pleiades. I read that
astronomers believed the star cluster formed from the
same gas/dust cloud about 100 million years ago. Other
studies said the stars are physically related and move as

a group, but they won't be held together by gravity forever and will eventually disperse. Though described as blue-white, a NASA image shows the stars as being of various colors, including orange--the star I'd chosen to observe is called Alcyone.

Next, I visited a music website and listened to the notes of the musical scale. The tone I remembered hearing was, indeed, D. Eastern healing teachings connect that note with the human body's sacral chakra. Interestingly the sacral chakra, the center of creativity, supposedly glows with orange light.

CHAPTER 28

As I'd done each morning since finishing high school, I put in my contact lenses so I could see my way through the day. Every lens storage case I'd used, for as long as I could remember, had an R on the right lid. The new one I'd just acquired featured a heart on the left lid.

The R means Ron is right, I heard him say in a playful tone. *The heart means Love, Ron. Just another way to get your attention. We spirits have to use all sorts of tricks and techniques to get humans to pay attention.*

Oddly, my eyesight has been improving over the past few years, at a stage in life when I would have expected it to worsen.

That's because you're starting to see more clearly at a non-physical level. You're stripping away the layers of illusion that cloud awareness, and that lets you see things you never realized were there before. Expanding your inner sight enhances your physical sight too.

Why hadn't I considered that possibility? I knew enough about holistic health to understand how much our thoughts and emotions can cause physical ailments. Healing the body often requires mental and emotional healing. I'd long suspected that the nearsightedness I'd known since childhood had its roots in my desire to avoid seeing situations in my early life.

The illusions we cling to act like cataracts, dulling the beauty around us and blinding us to the reality of existence. For me, the reverse was transpiring. Eagerly, I sought to see beyond the limits of ordinary vision, beyond the material world. Apparently, my intention had produced results on more than one level.

"Are you healing me?" I asked Ron, as I spooned coffee beans into the grinder and whirred them down to dark, fragrant grounds, then filled the coffeemaker's receptacle with water.

You're healing yourself. Spirits lend a hand at times, though.

"You put ideas into doctors' heads, right?"

Sometimes.

Several years ago, Ron had his right hip replaced. While he was in surgery, I walked the labyrinth at the local Episcopal Church and envisioned a successful outcome. Ron's doctor later told me he'd received an insight in the midst of the operation and decided to try a new technique that made the process easier. I like to think spirits or guides--Ron's and/or mine--assisted the surgeon.

Spirits help humans, but humans can help spirits too, Ron said.

"How?"

By sending us love. Love is the answer to every problem, on earth and elsewhere.

Dr. Bernie Siegel wrote in his book *Love, Medicine and Miracles,* "I am convinced that unconditional love is the most powerful known stimulant to the immune system . . . The truth is: love heals." In my opinion, that's the secret of Reiki's effectiveness.

The Reiki helped ease my passage, Ron told me after he reached the other side. *You can still send it to me, you know. I don't need a physical body to get the benefits.*

"Okay, I will," I promised.

And another thing. I wish you'd stop mourning me. I don't like to see you sad. Those of us over here want our loved ones to hold on to happy thoughts about us. Remember the good times we had together, instead of thinking about me lying in that hospital bed or thinking I'm gone. You know better.

I did, but I was still having trouble adjusting to this shift in our relationship. After pouring coffee into a mug, I carried it out to the back porch while Henry Scott Holland's poem ran through my mind. I tried to imagine Ron in the next room, around the corner, just out of sight. Some people, I knew, refrained from even talking about their deceased loved ones or spoke of them only in hushed, sorrowful tones. For me, talking and writing about Ron brought comfort and seemed to strengthen our connection. Pictures of him graced my living and dining rooms, office, and bedroom.

"What else can I do?" I asked.

Play music for me.

Ron loved Pavarotti's music. He'd attended several of the tenor's concerts and met with the maestro once, during which they had a brief conversation in Italian. When Pavarotti passed, Ron prepared the singer's favorite meal and we drank an exquisite, forty-year-old bottle of Amarone in honor of Luciano. We dined by candlelight, listening to the great man's incomparable voice. He'll continue to enchant listeners long after his soul has moved on to other venues.

That's something else you can do for me. Eat and drink things I liked. I don't have sensory organs where I am now, but I can still enjoy food and wine through you. It's not quite the same, but close enough.

"Really? How does that work?"

We're not separate, as I keep telling you. I can feel what you're feeling. When you enjoy something, I experience your pleasure.

"What do you want me to eat and drink for you?"

Good California cabs. Peaty, smoky scotch--I left some Lagavulin in the kitchen closet. Steak. Lobster. Osso bucco. Smoked Norwegian salmon. Reggiano parmesano. Gorgonzola. Pistachio nuts. Crème brulee.

"Okay, I'm making a list. No gorgonzola though."

How can you not like gorgonzola? he teased. *If I'd known a congenital brain anomaly would be my downfall, I'd have stopped worrying about calories, fat, sugar, and all that other "unhealthy" stuff and eaten everything I wanted--I might have gained 200 pounds. I would've smoked cigarettes and quit working out too.*

"Maybe it's not only about what contributes to your death, but how well you live while you're in the physical world," I suggested. "Except for your sports-related injuries, you made it to sixty-nine without any significant health problems."

Other than a killer arteriovenus malformation, you mean?"

"Would you have wanted to know about that in advance?"

I'm glad I didn't, although knowing might have led me to behave better, to be kinder, more considerate, to treasure every moment we spent together instead of wasting so much time on things that didn't matter. Again, I regretted all the hurtful words I'd spoken, all the ways I'd shown disrespect, all the times I'd given in to fear and ego when I could have chosen love instead.

You can negate all that, if you want to, I heard him say. *You don't have to wait until your next lifetime to make amends. Remember I told you that you could change the past?*

He'd advised me to think about an experience I wished we'd handled better, and then to envision it surrounded by pink light, infusing the scenario with unconditional love. For some reason, I'd neglected to do this on a regular basis.

Allow the stress of the moment to dissipate as the light of love realigns the energies of that moment.

"I'll try."

Good girl. Now go in and eat your breakfast.

A few days later my friend Lyndsey explained a practice called recapitulation that Carlos Castaneda had written about in the 1960s and 1970s. Supposedly it neutralized energies that might otherwise taint, block, or convolute one's spiritual path. Castaneda's method recommended that you inhale while contemplating an experience whose energies you wished to denature, release, or transform. As you slowly exhaled, you turned your head to the right and cast out the energy of the experience with your breath. This technique differed from what Ron had described, however the objective was similar.

The task seemed overwhelming. Even if I started right this minute, I could never undo all the negativity I'd already generated, never mind what I might sow tomorrow.

Just do your best. That's all you're ever asked to do, Ron assured me.

CHAPTER 29

On a gray, damp afternoon, I walked the three-mile roundtrip from our house to the mailbox, which I did a couple times a week. Dreary days like this made me feel sad--abundant sunshine was one of the best things about living in Texas. When Ron was physical, he and I walked this route regularly, as well as others around our ranch. Continuing to do the same things alone that we used to do together hadn't gotten any easier with the passing months. Every step I took reminded me of what I'd lost. Each day seemed endless and hopelessly bleak. How could I keep going on like this?

As tears welled up in my eyes, I felt his presence beside me. *If you really can't bear to go on, you can come over. I'll meet you,* he said. *I don't think it's a good idea, though. I know you feel shattered, but I'll help glue the pieces back together again.*

The image of him repairing me like a broken cup made me smile, despite my sadness, and I wiped my eyes.

You put so much thought and effort into arranging this lifetime--we both did--and you've spent so many years getting to this point, it would be a shame to throw the opportunity away now. He paused, waiting for me to reply. When I didn't, he continued. *I never wanted to hurt you. I thought I'd done the right thing by giving you the financial security you needed to finish the work you'd chosen to do.*

"I know, and I'm grateful," I said, and I meant it.

A hundred times a day I silently thanked him for all he'd done for me, not only for the material things he'd given me but all he'd taught me and shared with me as well. Still, the process of putting one foot in front of the other was almost more than I could manage. I tried repeating the Alcoholics Anonymous phrase "one day at a time" but sometimes I felt incapable of enduring even one more hour. The thought of slogging on like this for years seemed impossible.

I realized many people considered suicide a sin, one serious enough to consign a soul to hell and eternal damnation. They believed taking one's own life was morally wrong and such an act required punishment. If, as some religions teach, life on earth is a gift from God and He puts us here for a reason, people who kill themselves are disobeying God and throwing the gift back in His face.

Although I didn't believe all that, I agreed suicide probably wasn't a good idea, even though leaving earth held immense appeal for me right now. How I longed to relax in the peaceful, joyous realm I'd visited with Ron, a place where love prevailed. Where anger, hate, and fear were only vague, distant memories.

Ron interrupted my ruminations. *The "punishment" is having to experience during life review how your actions affected everyone who loved you. You'd be surprised how many people care about you, baby, and how much it would hurt them if you checked yourself out. That's the main reason I didn't shoot myself, even though I wanted to--I couldn't do that to you.*

Tears ran down my cheeks as I remembered how he'd talked about "eating a bullet" and my attempts to persuade him not to do it, telling him how devastated I'd be, how much I'd miss him. His passing due to natural causes was heartbreaking enough; to lose him to suicide would have been unbearable.

Besides, it doesn't solve anything. In another lifetime you'd have to finish what you left undone in this one, perhaps under less advantageous conditions. Plus you'd have the added responsibility of balancing the suffering you caused this time around. Of course, it's your choice.

Dr. Raymond Moody, in *Reflections on Life After Life,* wrote something similar. Patients he'd regressed with hypnosis to past lifetimes when they'd killed themselves all agreed "their suicidal attempts solved nothing." According to Moody, they faced the same problems they'd tried to escape by suicide. "Whatever difficulty they had been trying to get away from was still on the other side, unresolved."

I reached the mailbox and pulled out an assortment of junk mail, two bills, and a catalog for pet supplies that triggered feelings of grief for my beloved cat, Domino.

Don't take the material world so seriously and you'll feel better, Ron said as I stuffed the mail into my canvas tote bag. *When you're not embodied you don't feel pain or fear or sorrow. I can remember I was sad on earth, but I don't feel it now. It's sort of like a nightmare you remember when you wake up, but it doesn't scare you anymore.*

I slid the straps of my tote bag over my shoulder. "That's easy for you to say, you don't have to live here anymore."

The physical world is just a tiny piece in the whole scheme of things. I've been trying to show you that. This lifetime on earth is only one piece of a giant jigsaw puzzle and you can't understand the big picture by looking at only one piece.

• • •

In the days that followed, I tried to accept that life on earth is supposed to be hard, that we learn through facing challenges. By overcoming difficulties, we grow stronger. It was like working with a physical trainer-- you had to keep pushing a little more every day if you wanted to improve. Intellectually, I got it, but in my heart I still resisted.

Think about the heroine in your book, Ron said, referring to a mystery novel I was writing. *She has to go through all sorts of turmoil, trials, and danger in order to figure out what's going on and solve the mystery. In the process, she also finds out what she's made of. That's what humans do, too, in their daily lives.*

That's why people love reading mysteries. They're not only morality tales, in which the bad guys get their come-uppance. Mysteries are modern-day versions of the hero/ine's journey into the frightening, unknown realms. As in old myths, the protagonist faces demons in the outer world and in herself, and comes out the victor.

Like your heroine, Ron continued, *human beings go through trials to test their metal. Don't think of it as onerous. You're trying out things to see what you're capable of and what might happen if you do this or that. You're shifting pieces around, seeing things from different perspectives. Like looking through a kaleidoscope. You adjust the bits of glass, not knowing what pattern will result, and let the light shine through. You can create an endless variety of possibilities. Of course, the images you see are illusions.*

I sensed him laughing and patting me on the head affectionately. *It's a game. Try to see it as an adventure.*

He was right, but I didn't want to learn anything more. I wanted to rest. I longed for peace. Maybe I should check myself into the ruby-red world Ron showed me during one of our early journeys for some R&R.

When you're human, you tend to connect love with loss, he said. *On earth, everything is finite, everything ends sooner or later. You're so afraid of losing what you love that you only open the door to your heart a crack, instead of throwing it wide open and welcoming love in.*

After a few painful losses, you might bolt the door shut permanently. I don't want you to do that, baby. When you shut love out, you also shut the pain in. You make things harder for yourself. Your job--everyone's job-- is to help one another, to try to make life easier and happier. As Ram Dass said, "We're all just walking each other home."

His description fit me perfectly. I'd slammed the door to my heart shut. I couldn't imagine ever opening it to another man--I hadn't even adopted another cat yet, and good cats were a lot easier to find than good men. I recalled the image of me as a broken cup. Even if Ron somehow managed to glue me back together again the cracks would remain.

Have you ever heard about a Japanese art called Kintsugi? he asked.

"No, what is it?"

It's a technique for repairing broken objects. The artisan mixes resin with powered gold, or another precious metal, and then uses it as a glue to stick the pieces back together. Instead of hiding the cracks, this method emphasizes them--the cracks become a distinctive and beautiful part of the whole. Try to think of yourself as human Kintsugi. Cracked, yes, but more beautiful for the experience.

CHAPTER 30

One night I dreamed about trying on an assortment of bracelets. Ordinarily, I would have interpreted the dream as my subconscious experimenting with various lifestyles or ideas. When I woke up, however, Ron's bracelet--the one I'd worn since his last day in the hospital--was gone. Aghast, I stripped the bed and shook out the sheets, hoping it had gotten caught in the bedding. No bracelet. Where could it be . . . I never took it off . . . surely it was securely fastened on my wrist when I went to bed . . . ?

As I frantically searched the bedroom, I heard Ron singing *unchain your heart,* a variation on the old Ray Charles song.

"Did you take it?" I asked.

He'd manifested a piece of rose quartz for me to find, toyed with my computer, and caused electric lights to blink on and off repeatedly. I didn't doubt he could hide the bracelet from me.

Don't chain yourself to me.

The silver bracelet, which our jeweler friend Leslie had made for him decades ago, was a series of links hooked together to form a chain.

"Give it back," I demanded.

That's not your only link to me, he said, another play on words. *No object can bind us together, no material loss can weaken our connection.* Then he started singing Aretha Franklin's hit "Chain, Chain, Chain."

I sat on the bed and started to cry. "Give it back," I pleaded.

Stop clinging to the past. You have too much to do in the next few years.

Although I knew he meant to get my attention and make a point, I was in no mood for games. Three days later I found the bracelet lying in the driveway. I still can't come up with a rational explanation for how it got there.

• • •

After the bracelet incident, I began to examine the concept of attachment, or chains, as Ron put it. Although I didn't know much about Buddhism, I knew that Buddhists consider attachment to be a cause of human suffering. Fundamental to Buddhist teachings are premises known as the Four Noble Truths.

The First Noble Truth says that life on earth is suffering, a sense of dissatisfaction and discontent due to our ignorance of the truth. We're unhappy because we think we're separate from other beings and things, which is a misconception.

The Second Noble Truth explains that this feeling of separation leads us to form attachments in the mistaken belief that doing so will provide security and connection. As humans, we attach to all sorts of things: possessions, power, beliefs and ideologies, our careers, other people, a culture or country.

The Third Noble Truth tells us it's possible to end suffering by letting go of attachments, as well as the emotions, ideas, and illusions associated with them. Through nonattachment, we can reach a state of joyful freedom known as nirvana.

The Fourth Noble Truth presents a guideline for living, known as the Eightfold Path, designed to end human suffering.

According to the Zen teacher John Daido Loori, detachment and separation are not the same. In fact, they're opposites. He reminds us that everything in the universe is connected. "If you have unified with the whole universe, there's nothing outside of you, so the notion of attachment becomes absurd."

While he was still on earth, Ron had vehemently rejected all religions and he probably knew even less about Buddhism than I did. Yet some of what he'd described since going home sounded very much like the first three Noble Truths. As I contemplated these ideas, I sensed him touch my hair and knew he'd stopped by for a visit.

The purpose is to eliminate suffering, on earth and elsewhere, he said. *The more we understand, the less we suffer.*

I wondered, is that what the Dalai Lama meant when he said the purpose of life is to be happy? Ron had said souls don't come to earth to be happy, but maybe that outcome was possible if we could let go of fear and attachment.

Our lives become better and easier as we learn more, Ron continued. *This can manifest in physical terms, such as good health, greater comfort, fewer burdens and limitations, though that's not always the case. In some cases, "better" means an expanded sense of peace or contentment.*

I recalled the vast number of white souls I'd seen on my trip to Ron's home. "Beginners" he'd called them. Some of those young souls might take on lifetimes in which they suffered material hardships and limited freedom, as I had in earlier incarnations, in order to learn the rudiments of earthly existence.

However, suffering afflicted people at every station of life, in both external and internal ways--and, if the Buddhists were correct, misunderstanding lay at the root of all suffering. What about the powerful people at the top of the financial pyramid? Feeling isolated from the rest of the world, unable to trust the loyalty or intentions of those around them, afraid of losing the wealth and possessions they'd amassed. Their suffering might take a different, though no less painful form.

All the wars fought for material gain, I lamented. All the lives lost due to ideological misconceptions . . . it seemed so senseless and sad.

Earth life is basically a lucid dream, Ron explained. *Once you realize it's a dream, you can control and direct it. You're doing it all the time, directing your life with your thoughts. It's more obvious where I am, because we instantly see the results of our thoughts, but it's just as true for you on earth. Life isn't static, and what's more, it's not objective. What you see, feel, and believe are merely agreed upon standards, not the truth. You'll realize this immediately if you talk to someone from a different country or culture.*

He'd discussed some of these ideas with me before. In recent years, they'd become popularized as the Law of Attraction.

Furthermore, your existence is happening on many levels simultaneously. It's like a multi-level chess game. What you're aware of at any given moment is only a single level of its reality, and I don't mean this in psychological terms, although that's relevant too.

"So how are we mortals supposed to deal with life on earth, the illusions, the misconceptions, and the suffering that results?" I asked.

Keep in mind that earth is real and not real. It's physical, but not permanent. A good comparison is a stage set that allows actors to play out a scenario, but the set is just a prop. Your bodies, as we've talked about before, are like costumes that let you project the story-- they're physically real, but they're not you. Right now you're wearing the Skye suit, but you're much more than Skye.

Reincarnating into different bodies in different lifetimes is like playing various roles in a wide range of plays--each one tests your talents and gives you a chance to try out new possibilities. Souls like to experiment, which is one reason earthly incarnations are relatively short. In earlier times, when people's lives were tedious and limited, souls left their host bodies sooner. They got bored. Now that more options for growth exist, souls are choosing to stick around longer in physical forms in order to experience more, although a lifetime on earth is still only a blink of an eye in the whole scheme of things.

Most of the lifetimes I'd revisited in my regressions fell into the category of tedious and limited. Peasant, housemaid, slave, powerless child. The ones I'd spent in convents, translating and copying manuscripts, had allowed me to expand my intellectual abilities. But they didn't offer any opportunities to experience the larger world, or the intricacies of love and romantic relationships, or the challenges of handling financial matters and property. Was it possible I'd lived more exciting and glamorous existences at some time in the past, but hadn't yet discovered them?

I have to leave now to play football, Ron said. *Before I go I want to tell you one more thing. Earth has been designed to help souls grow, and we've all participated to some extent in the planet's creation. It will exist as long as we need it to further our growth. When all souls have learned what earth can offer, when everyone "gets it" and love prevails, the planet will be dismantled. Earth will disappear.*

• • •

Several days later while rummaging through piles of old paperwork stashed in boxes I hadn't opened in years, I came upon a folded sheet of paper, brittle and yellowed with age. I opened it carefully and read the words written there by a man I'd met in Greece in 1971. Michael was one of the most enigmatic and charismatic people I've ever encountered. A white Englishman, he'd walked away from his home in South Africa seven years earlier, in repudiation of Apartheid. He'd been traveling the world ever since, without money, and with only the barest of belongings that he could carry on his back. For four days I lived with him in a cave on one of Greece's beautiful islands, before he moved on to continue his sojourn.

As my eyes scanned the piece of paper I'd totally forgotten about, I read words that were even more poignant now than they'd been at the time Michael wrote them:

"When the power of love
Replaces the love of power,
Man will have a new name:
God." -- Sri Chinmoy

• • •

That evening as I sat down to dinner, Ron made his presence known by singing Huey Lewis's "The Power of Love." I lifted my wineglass in a toast to him and invited him to join me at the table.

Love of power is a huge problem among human beings, he said, referring to the note I'd found from my long-ago friend Michael. *And not only today. It's ever been thus.*

Recently I'd read a book about the Borgias in Renaissance Italy and their ruthless machinations to seize and hold power in Europe at that time. Humans' vainglorious quest for wealth and domination was no worse in centuries past than today, we're just capable of greater destruction now.

It's been one my problems too, Ron continued. *Can you remember our lifetime in Austria in the seventeenth century? I was a cardinal then--a corrupt one, as many were--and you were an abbess at a small and insignificant convent. You were a thorn in my side, always criticizing me for what you considered my wanton behavior, but outside the convent you had no power. I could've had you chastened, but I admired your feistiness and determination. You were like a kitten hissing at a wolf, yet you never backed down.*

The picture of him wearing a scarlet robe and me dressed in a wimple made me laugh. "Is that why you show yourself as a cardinal now?" I asked, meaning the bird that visited me.

Glad you caught on to that. It's also one reason why I had such rancor toward the Church and politics in my lifetime as Ron--and why you do too. Neither of us has any tolerance for hypocrisy or bogus authority.

I poked at my lasagna, a frozen packaged meal I'd heated up, not like the delicious ones Ron made from scratch. "How can we combat the power-hungry?"

Ordinary people now, as then, seemed helpless to check the rule of the mighty in business, politics, and religion.

By searching out your own desire for power, wherever that may manifest, and stepping back from it. You can't dislodge something in the outer world until you recognize it in yourself and root it out.

CHAPTER 31

Lesson for today, listen up, Ron greeted me playfully, like a teacher calling his class to order. He would have been a wonderful, though strict teacher and I was grateful for what he'd taught me.

I saved what I'd worked on all afternoon--research for a historical mystery novel I planned to write--and stepped away from my computer. "Okay, I've done enough for one day."

It's a good thing you have a lot of quiet time these days. If you were working a nine-to-five job you'd never hear me for all the noise. Staying busy is a good way to avoid looking at things deeply, yourself included.

Maybe he was right. The loneliness I viewed as a deficit, he considered a plus. People on spiritual paths often sequestered themselves in ashrams or embarked on vision quests alone, in order to escape the busyness of the everyday world and to hear the voice of wisdom that abides in silence. Perhaps I should try to see my life in that way.

Human lifetimes are divided into four parts: those of the body, the mind, the heart, and the soul, Ron explained.

Usually, we think of our lives in terms of youth, maturity, and old age. Goddess-based spirituality calls them maiden, mother, and crone. The categories he described made no sense to me.

I'm referring to areas of primary focus, where your greatest growth takes place. For many people, the first two decades are the time of the body. Obviously, you're going through all kinds of physical growth and changes during this stage as you evolve from infant to adult. But some people's focus on the body stage comes later, during pregnancy or menopause, for example, or as a result of a physical illness or infirmity. In this period, you learn the lessons of the body, its pleasures and limitations. You learn how to exist as an infinite soul within the confines of the finite world.

I poured myself a glass of chianti and carried it outside to the porch. I sat in my favorite spot, where I could look out at the distant hills and watch the puffy white clouds drift by. Back in Massachusetts, the trees would be turning yellow, orange, and red now. Here in Texas, however, fall was a lackluster event that would ease into next month without fanfare.

"This sounds like an interesting class," I said. "Do go on."

The second stage, although it may not occur in the second part of your earth life or follow the body stage consecutively, is the time of the mind. At this stage, you concentrate on developing your mental abilities. For some people, this happens during their school years; for others, the mind phase equates with the middle part of their lives when they're developing their career skills and exercising their knowledge in the larger world. *Still others may devote themselves to mental activities after they retire and have time to explore their ideas and interests at length.*

As I sipped my wine, several black buck antelope cruised through my property, gracefully trotting and leaping across the rugged terrain as if their delicate legs were joined with springs. I shifted my attention to these beautiful creatures momentarily, and wondered if Ron, too, admired them from his perspective.

The third phase, he continued, *is that of the heart. During this stage you open yourself to love and engage your emotions deeply, passionately, allowing them to take precedence over everything else. Again, this can happen at any chronological age. For many people, the heart phase occurs relatively early in life, during their twenties or thirties, but it can happen later--perhaps after a midlife divorce or even in old age, when a person is facing the loss of a partner.*

"You ushered in my heart phase," I told him.

I'd had a number of romantic relationships during my youth and had been married for twenty-five years to a man I still considered a friend. But I'd never loved anyone as intensely and passionately as I loved Ron. As he'd described, my focus during our time together was awakening to love and all that entailed. With him, I'd known the heights and the depths the heart can reach, beyond anything I'd previously imagined to be possible.

A saying from the Chinese sage Lao Tzu came to mind: "Being deeply loved by someone gives you strength, loving someone deeply gives you courage."

And now you're in the soul phase.

It certainly seemed that way. Since his transition from the realm of earth to that of spirit, I'd focused almost exclusively on the afterlife and other levels of existence beyond the physical one we usually accept as "reality." In the process, most of the concerns I'd previously placed front and center--career success, creature comforts, financial security, health, beauty-- had taken a backseat. I'd become obsessed with understanding my soul's purpose, my connection with higher planes of awareness, and how each thought and action affected my spiritual progress.

Perhaps this was typical for people late in life, whose loved ones have gone on ahead and who are struggling to make sense of their perceived losses. In Western society, at least, the end phase doesn't seem very desirable, particularly when viewed in terms of material standards. A good many people, I dare say, have sought spiritual solace in their "declining" days.

However, as I understood it, we needn't relegate the soul stage to the last years of human life. Some children are keenly aware of their souls' continued existence, as past-life researchers attest--the movie *Little Buddha* presents a good example. Joan of Arc and Teresa of Avila began experiencing divine revelations while they were still in their teens. During the 1960s and '70s, many young people--including luminaries such as the Beatles--journeyed to India and other mystical places, endeavoring to expand their spiritual lives.

Of the four stages Ron had outlined, this one seemed likely to be the most enduring. Even when it no longer held primary focus for the individual, the lessons one learned during this period continued to influence the rest of that person's life.

As I watched the big Texas sky gradually shift from light blue to turquoise, the clouds from creamy white to purple, I tried to embrace this stage of my life that promised untold riches. If only I could open myself to receive them.

"Does everyone go through all four stages in every lifetime?"

No, and most people aren't aware of the growth they're undergoing at the time it's happening.

I had to admit I'd never thought of the passages in my life in this way before, nor had I come across this concept in the many books on spirituality and self-help I'd read over the years. As I mentally flipped through my past lives, I couldn't find even one in which I'd undergone all four stages.

Many of my incarnations had been brief, however, ending while I was still just a child. As an adolescent housemaid and later as a boy traveling through the American West in a wagon train, my only concern had been physical survival: the body stage. During my cloistered lifetimes I'd embraced the stages of mind and soul, but never the heart phase. I felt a new appreciation for my life as Skye and the opportunities granted me this time around. In this incarnation, I was fortunate to have the chance to experience all four.

After Ron finished telling me about these life stages, I went back to my computer and recorded what he'd said. While I typed the words, a male cardinal landed on the fence in front of the house, outside my office window, and I sensed Ron's approval--of me *and* the new fence.

CHAPTER 32

During the next few days, I continued contemplating the four stages of life and growth Ron had described to me. One evening, I leafed through the book *Seth Speaks,* a collection of communications between a disincarnate entity named Seth and a human channel named Jane Roberts. As synchronicity would have it, the book fell open to a page where Seth mentioned a lifetime he'd chosen to take as a beggar, after having experienced many incarnations of indulgence and hedonism.

Souls choose earth lifetimes they believe will fill in gaps in their growth process, Ron explained. *This time, you chose to emphasize love and relationships, an area you hadn't developed in previous incarnations. You opted to accelerate your growth by undergoing a childhood full of emotional landmines and picking romantic partners who'd challenge your ability to keep your heart open.*

"Then I guess I should thank you for putting me through my paces, right?" I said, trying not to sound sarcastic.

It was an agreement we made together. Yes, I admit I was hard on you at times, but look how much you've learned as a result. People mistakenly believe soul

*mates enjoy blissful, harmonious lives together, happy-
ever-after and all that Disney stuff, but it's not true. Soul
mates force you to confront your fears, your limits, your
strengths, and your possibilities. A relationship with a
soul mate is one of the toughest you'll ever face, but
also the most rewarding.*

In her book *Eat, Pray, Love,* Elizabeth Gilbert
points out, "A soul mate's purpose is to shake you up,
tear apart your ego a little bit, show you your obstacles
and addictions, break your heart open so new light can
get in, make you so desperate and out of control that
you have to transform your life."

Marianne Williamson, in *A Return to Love*--a
book that literally fell off a shelf and landed at my feet-
-writes, "People who have the most to teach us are
often the ones who reflect back to us the limits of our
own capacity to love." In addition, she says, "If a
relationship lasts, it will demand all of our skills at
compassion, acceptance, release, forgiveness, and
selflessness."

Ron had done all that for me, and more.

• • •

I'd often heard religious and spiritual teachers say God
never gives us more hardship than we can handle, but I
wasn't sure about that. The old saying "What doesn't
kill you makes you stronger" arose in my mind too.
Was inhabiting earth merely an endurance test? It sure
felt that way at times.

As I slogged up a hill on my afternoon walk to the mailbox, I sensed Ron fall in beside me.

In between earth lives, souls tend to forget how hard it is to be physical, he admitted.

"Like childbirth you mean?" I asked. "People forget how excruciatingly painful it is and then go on to do it again?"

I heard him chuckle at my analogy. *Sometimes, when we're planning our next incarnations, we believe we can manage more than is humanly possible because we don't feel pain or the limitations of embodiment here. We think, yeah, I can handle that--bring it on. Plus, we can see the big picture--we know we'll only inhabit earth for a short period of time and then we'll come back to this beautiful place, so no problem.*

"Except once the soul enters a body all the harsh realities of earth-life hit you like an eighteen-wheeler, right?"

Pretty much, he agreed. *Sometimes life in the physical world really is too hard.*

"No wonder newborns cry at birth."

When we're at home, disembodied, we're immersed in unconditional love--it's the very nature of our existence. We don't have emotions like humans do. Love, human-style, bears little resemblance to the real deal. Human relationships are a murky mishmash of idealism, ego, fantasy, desire, projection, fear, power struggles, self-aggrandizement, and self-annihilation.

"Don't I know it," I grumbled.

253

You can't learn unconditional love while you're surrounded by it, though, Ron continued. *You should be glad you feel pain.*

At the top of the long hill, I paused momentarily to catch my breath. "How so?"

It means you're accomplishing what you planned to do in this lifetime. You wanted to experience strong emotions during your incarnation as Skye. It's like exercising--the aching muscles let you know you've had a good work out.

"No pain, no gain, as they say."

Want me to tell you a story?

I shrugged. "Sure, why not?"

The concept of romantic love that Western people still subscribe to today dates back to the late medieval period in Europe. In those days, marriages were arranged for practical, financial, or political reasons-- love played no part in it. To fill the emotional void, a formalized system of "courtly love" rose up among members of the royal and noble classes. According to the rules of this system, a highborn lady set her sights on a knight and granted him her favor. He swore to honor and cherish her, and he carried her standard into battle. They adored and admired one another, but their love wasn't supposed to be consummated. She was married to someone else, someone in a position of power who held their lives in the palm of his hand. Of course, the Church considered infidelity a mortal sin.

"For women anyway. Sounds like a prescription for infinite frustration and heartbreak."

You once were a lady of noble standing in Belgium--not royalty, but positioned well enough to take part in the ridiculous farce, Ron continued. *You took a fancy to me--I was a handsome and much-admired knight who'd made a name for himself with acts of bravery. You claimed me as your champion.*

This wasn't an existence I'd encountered during my past-life regressions. Among the many humble, bleak, and dull lifetimes I'd recollected, this one promised a bit of glamour. I was eager to hear more.

But you belonged to another man, and I garnered the attention of many women from the highest to the lowest classes. In previous lifetimes, I'd been a chieftain, a warlord, a leader who took what he wanted without regard for "rules"--I made the rules. You, on the other hand, subscribed to the intricate etiquette and dictates of the court. So although I was your suitor, I refused to limit myself to a chaste relationship with a woman who treated me like her pet.

When I embarrassed you by taking up with other women, including your sister, you had your husband send me away to war, where I was killed. Having to go on living without me, mired in pride, misery, and guilt, broke your heart. You spent a long string of lifetimes after that avoiding emotional entanglements so you wouldn't get hurt again.

I reached the mailbox and pulled out an invoice for my car insurance, an ad for new windows, and a card inviting me to a free dinner if I listened to a spiel about hearing aids. Memories of Ron's amorous flirtations swirled in my mind. I realized his inconsequential indiscretions that I found so hurtful and humiliating in this life might have been rooted in the heartbreaking shame that took place hundreds of years ago.

That ancient wounds could continue to ache and influence our actions in the here-and-now amazed and confounded me. Not only did we have to deal with the seemingly overwhelming challenges of the present, but also demons from the past that we're largely unaware of.

How could we humans possibly bear up under the strain? Each lifetime layered on even more karmic conditions that required balancing. The whole business was starting to seem like cosmic usury. With so much "past" clinging to us like barnacles, how could we ever hope to dig out of the muck and move ahead? How could we even be sure what we felt in the present wasn't an aftershock of the past?

Ron read my mind and answered, *By washing away the grime of illusion so you can see the love you knew before you took human form. It's easier than you think--love is what you're made of. It's your natural state of being. Everything else is artifice.*

Then he quoted from a Rumi poem--something he never would have done while in the person of Ron:

"Keep knocking, and the joy inside

*will eventually open a window
and look out to see who's there."*

• • •

It was still dark outside when I sensed Ron standing beside my bed. I opened my eyes and saw him glowing softly in the shadows of the bedroom. Although he appeared humanlike, the edges of his form were fuzzy and I could see through him. As he climbed into bed with me, I felt a flicker of apprehension.

I didn't mean to startle you, he said. *I come to you like this a lot, but usually you don't see me or you think it's just a dream. I always liked sleeping with you when I was physical.*

Still confused, I remembered smelling his scent at night occasionally or feeling a gentle breeze from an unknown source caress my cheek.

"I'm glad you're here," I said.

Go back to sleep now.

CHAPTER 33

Can you take a break? Ron asked.

I'd spent the afternoon doing research for my new book about fairy mythology, reading dozens of stories, legends, and accounts of fairy sightings from around the world. Keeping busy helped me get through the days. Besides, I found the folklore about these elusive beings fascinating.

Remember the day we met? You told me fairies lived in your backyard. I thought you were crazy. Cute, but crazy.

"And now?"

Fairies seem pretty ordinary in the whole scheme of things.

I saved the document I'd been working on and closed the file. "Okay, what's up?"

I thought we could take a trip together. How about visiting another solar system? I'll take you to the World of Yellow Sky. It's not physical, so scientists don't know it exists. The universe is full of such places.

"You're on," I agreed.

I settled myself comfortably in the big, overstuffed chair I used for meditation and slowly relaxed into a trance. After several minutes, I felt my consciousness lifting away from my body. I floated beside Ron in darkness for a while, until finally we entered a soft, thick, yellowish fog that encased us completely. No land, nothing solid. Just dense, mustard-colored light. Above, I noticed a band of deep purple clouds, as if a storm were approaching.

A faint whirring, like the sound of thousands of tiny wings beating, filled the space and I became aware of swarms of infinitesimal things flying around me. I couldn't actually feel them--I simply knew they were there. First I imagined they might be insects, but then thought it could be a whirlwind of yellow sand.

That buzzing can't be heard by physical ears, Ron pointed out.

I glanced around, squinting, trying to see beyond the dull yellow fog or dust cloud or whatever this was. Below us I spotted an indigo circle that looked like a hole.

It's a tunnel, he explained. *We can travel through it to go to another place if you find this one uncomfortable.*

We decided to slide through the hole, into a cavern blacker than the night sky. All I could see was a thin, greenish rim glowing at the end of the passageway, but I vaguely sensed the presence of primitive life forms hunkered down in the darkness. Before I could wonder what they might be, we'd whizzed through the cavern and emerged into a bright, blue, watery world.

This is the Place of Water, Ron said. *It's a small "planet" composed completely of water.*

I felt myself bobbing up and down and heard the roar of waves that swelled, crested, and broke on some indiscernible shore. Sunlight glinted off the water and made my eyes hurt. Shielding my eyes with my hand, I observed that the planet, instead of being round, was oblong and flattened on the top and bottom, like old-fashioned images of flying saucers.

Here the sun shines all the time, there's no night. Of course, none of it's physical yet--the planet won't be "discovered" for a while.

"Are you saying it will eventually become physical?" I asked.

When its energy grows dense enough--or when it becomes necessary to support life elsewhere or to benefit the evolution of the cosmos. That's how planets come into being.

I contemplated the idea for a moment. "You mean that before astronomers discover a planet, the planet isn't really there? It's not just because their telescopes aren't strong enough to see it?"

Right. We weren't ready to "see" Pluto before 1930, but its energy was operating all along and influenced the 1929 stock market crash. Remember the first chapter in Genesis about the earth being without form and void, and the Spirit of God moving on the face of the waters? Then He creates light, and dry land, and the rest of it?

"Yes, so . . ."

Where he was going with this discussion? During the time we'd spent together, Ron had known nothing about astrology and expressed nothing but distain for religion. Before I had a chance to ask, however, he replied to my questions.

You know how I feel about religion. But that quote uses symbolism to describe what really happened in earth's emergence, albeit in a much abbreviated way. The same thing will occur here one day, on the Place of Water. It's fluid and without substance now, but that will change, as happened with earth. Planets go through evolutionary periods, just as species on planets do. Everything, everywhere is in a constant state of development, growth and disintegration, birth and death.

The ideas intrigued me and I decided to revisit one we'd touched upon before. "Is earth real, or not?"

Both. It has substance, but it's also an illusion. It exists, but only so long as its purpose lasts. It's not permanent. Earth gives souls a place to experiment with material existence, among other things. All of us created it and continue creating it, all the time, with our thoughts and emotions. It would disintegrate if humans stopped believing in it and needing it.

"It's all so confusing."

Only because your perspective is narrow. Anyplace else you want to go?

"Not today," I answered. "I'm feeling overwhelmed as it is."

Okay, I'll take you back.

After I settled into my body and got my "earth legs" again, I wrote down everything I could remember of the trip. Then I phoned my friend Lyndsey to tell her about it.

"Oh my god," she exclaimed. "That sounds like the 'yellow sulfur world' Carlos Castenada wrote about."

"You mean someone else has been there?"

"Google it and see what you can find."

What I read online closely matched what I'd witnessed in the World of Yellow Sky. The yellowish fog, the flying specks, the buzzing. One website said that something called "inorganic beings" stored their offspring and valuables in the dark, cave-like tunnel Ron and I had traveled through. Those, I assumed, must be the life forms I'd sensed inside. Amazing! But no more amazing than the rest of my experiences. Still, it provided affirmation. I smiled to myself, thinking, either I'm not crazy, or a bunch of other people are just as whacko as me.

As I continued reading, I came upon something called an "assemblage point." According to the writer, every human being is surrounded by a cocoon of energy that emanates from the body. Supposedly, lines crisscross this cocoon like a web. Somewhere along those lines exists the person's assemblage point, and through that point he or she perceives the world. I envisioned it as a tiny telescope.

In most people, the article said, rigid thinking keeps their assemblage points stuck, so they view the world in a limited way. However, if you slide your assemblage point along the web of lines to another place in the cocoon--aim the telescope lens in another direction--you can perceive the world in a completely different way. This, the writer explained, happens during dreams, meditation, trances states, the use of mind-altering substances, and various shamanic practices.

That's what Ron's teaching me, I realized. To shift my perception so I can see beyond the ordinary world and begin to answer the great questions in life. I made some notes, including the titles of a few books to check out. Such strange ideas, yet somehow they rang true.

As I left the website, I heard Ron's voice reciting a line from *Hamlet: "There are more things in heaven and earth, Horatio, than are dreamt of in your philosophy."*

CHAPTER 34

In November, I adopted a kitten from one of the local animal shelters, an adorable, five-month-old black Manx with Hemingway paws. Often I joked that what she lacked in tail she made up for in toes. She had a small splash of white like a brushstroke on her right hip. Domino had one in the same place--I recognized it as a sign that my feline friend had guided me to this new cat. I named her Zoe, which means "life" and "soul" in Greek.

Like people, animals have souls and reincarnate. Domino, I felt certain, was the reincarnation of a beloved cat named Izmir that had previously lived with me for eighteen years. People who'd known both cats sometimes called Domino by her predecessor's name. Now I wondered if Zoe might be the reincarnation of a sweet tuxedo cat named Magic, who'd lived with me years ago and disappeared on a bitter-cold winter day in Massachusetts.

Ron had told me animals of all kinds inhabited the afterlife, including long-extinct creatures and some that have not yet walked on earth. This belief, I realized, may not be widely accepted in contemporary Western society. However, the ancient Egyptians considered cats sacred. When a ruler died, that person's feline companions were mummified, too, and placed in the deceased's tomb, so they could accompany him or her into the afterlife.

The Egyptian pantheon even featured a cat goddess named Bast (or Bastet), along with numerous other deities who were human-animal hybrids. Many other cultures--among them the Hindus, Aztecs, Australian Aborigine, and the ancient Greeks and Romans--also recognized divine beings in animal, bird, reptile, or composite forms.

I tossed a crinkly ball made of metallic-foil for Zoe and watched her dash across the kitchen chasing it.

Every living thing has a soul, and everything is infinite, Ron's voice said. *I'm not just saying that to keep you from worrying that you'll never see your former pets again.*

Recently I'd heard Arizona psychic and medium Susanne Wilson say essentially the same thing in an interview on "Beyond Reality Radio." Bill D. Schul, in his book *Animal Immortality,* gives numerous examples of animal spirits that appeared to people. One, a white cat that had lived with the housekeeper of an English abbey, continued showing up for forty years after its physical death.

The indigenous people of North America speak of spirit animals--guides in the spirit realm who protect and instruct human beings--who appear to us in the guise of animals, birds, reptiles, and other creatures. According to some sources, these beings once existed on earth in physical forms and then passed into the spirit world after their bodies died. Others say spirits can assume the shapes of flesh-and-blood creatures when they choose and can journey through various realms of existence at will. The cardinals that show themselves to me seem to fit this description.

Zoe brought the crinkly ball back to me and I threw it for her again. How could animals *not* have souls? I wondered. If we want to see examples of pure love and generosity, of living without malice, we need only look to animals for guidance.

We're all sparks of the same consciousness-- Oneness, All-That-Is, God, Goddess, Source, whatever you want to call it, Ron said. *Nothing is disconnected from the whole. Everything, animal, vegetable, mineral, resonates with intelligence. People need to stop viewing themselves as separate and superior to the rest of creation. We're all part of a continuum too vast for ordinary linear thinking to comprehend.*

Crystal workers speak of crystal consciousness that enables gemstones to heal, transmit information, and more. The Druids believed trees were sentient beings. In *The Secret Life of Plants,* authors Peter Tompkins and Christopher Bird describe experiments conducted by polygraph expert Cleve Backster that showed plants not only expressed emotion, but also had memory and could recognize people.

When I was doing research for my book *Fairies: The Myths, Legends, & Lore,* I came across a Chinese legend that discussed a mountain known as Kw'en Lun. It's said that on this mystical mountain grew the Tree of Life, a magnificent tree 15,000 feet tall and 1,800 feet around its trunk. Once every 3,000 years the tree bore magical peaches that supposedly confered immortality on whoever ate them.

Scientists know the rings in a tree's trunk contain records of rainfall, temperature, and other weather conditions, Ron told me. *What they don't realize is that the wood also holds the history of everything the tree has experienced--the deaths of its neighbors, visits from animals and birds, interactions with humans, its fear during storms and fires and the assault of loggers. These old trees have witnessed all kinds of stuff.*

The idea fascinated me. A friend had told me that in Texas some trees were named for events that took place near them. The "Treaty Oak" in Austin got its moniker because Stephen Austin, "the father of Texas," signed a treaty beneath it. The "Wedding Oak" in San Saba has witnessed countless weddings. What stories could they tell if they could talk?

I tossed the tinsel ball for Zoe again, while I contemplated the many roles trees play in mythology and religion. Often they serve as conduits between earth and the world of spirit--the Kabbalah's Tree of Life, the Tree of Knowledge in the Garden of Eden, the Celts' World Tree, and the Norse tree Yggdrasil.

The Irish even based an alphabet and a system of divination, known as Ogham, on trees. According to the sixteenth-century German botanist Jacob Boehem, "God had hidden clues for humanity's betterment inside the design of every flower, leaf, fruit, and tree on earth."

"How can I discover what the trees know?" I asked Ron.

Ask them.

• • •

One evening while I stood in my kitchen, spooning cat food into Zoe's bowl, a grayish ball the consistency of thick smoke and about the size of a grapefruit flew across the room. As it zipped into the adjoining living room Zoe dashed after it, but it shot through an exterior wall and disappeared before she could catch it.

Anyone who's lived with cats or dogs knows animals have highly developed senses that enable them to perceive things people can't. According to a study done at City University London, cats and other animals can see ultraviolet light, which is beyond the spectrum of human vision. However, both Zoe and I had seen this peculiar apparition. Neither of us felt uneasy, though, or threatened by the object, whatever it was. Only curious.

The more you open your eyes and your mind, the more you'll see, I heard Ron say. *The universe is populated by all sorts of beings.* Again, I thought of Shakespeare's statement that there are many more things in heaven and earth than our ordinary minds can comprehend.

The incident with the smoky-gray sphere prompted me to consider mythic creatures that have perplexed and fascinated us for centuries: fairies, mermaids, ETs, Bigfoot, and unicorns to name a few. Despite a lack of physical evidence, the number of eyewitness accounts, along with a rich and abiding body of folklore from countries around the world, make it difficult to deny that entities who may not be flesh-and-blood do, indeed, exist. And they move among us whether or not we're aware of their presence.

• • •

During the next few days, I continued to contemplate the idea of intelligent life in other parts of the universe. On my journeys to Titan and the World of Yellow Sky, I'd sensed the presence of lifeforms, albeit primitive ones, living there. The most popular extraterrestrials, usually known as "grays," have intrigued earthlings for centuries. Some researchers even claim to have found rock art depicting these visitors from outer space dating back 10,000 years.

Plenty of "ETs" around and about, Ron told me as I drove into town to meet a friend for lunch. *Some come to explore earth, some go to other places in the cosmos. They don't fly here in spaceships, though. They travel via thought, the same way you and I did when we went to Mars and Titan.*

"Are they more advanced forms of life?"

Some are, some aren't.

Alien enthusiasts suggest ETs come in a variety of shapes and sizes, not only the familiar grays with their huge heads and scrawny little bodies. Ron read my mind and said, *They can present themselves in any way they want to. They create their forms just as we create ours. Sometimes they appear human.*

He'd told me before to be on the lookout for all kinds of spirits, angels, entities from the afterlife, or beings who'd never assumed physical forms, including some who masqueraded as people. Spirits of myriad types walked among us.

I recalled a "man" Lyndsey and I passed one day in the park whom we both agreed wasn't human, though we had no idea who or what he might actually be. Carlos Castenada discussed in his books something called "inorganic beings" that occupy a world parallel to ours. An inorganic being possesses awareness, but lacks an organism. We coexist with them, but we rarely interact because our levels of awareness are different. Years later, I would read a book titled *Children of the Matrix* by David Icke that described other strange life forms, including a ferocious species called reptilians.

"Why are they interested in us?" I asked Ron.

They're curious, like people are. As I understand it--and remember, I don't have this all figured out either--some of them are attracted to the strong emotions humans express. They want to "capture" the energy of our emotions--including love, which is more intense in human beings than in other forms of consciousness.

271

"They're looking for love in the wrong place," I grumbled.

When I considered the endless wars, violence, and cruelty that plagued our planet, it seemed hate not love dominated.

Not true. If love didn't live on earth neither would you or anything else. At home, where I am now, spirits exist in a state of unconditional love. But it's not the same as the emotional love humans feel because spirits don't face the same challenges people do. For us, love isn't a choice; there's no dilemma, it simply is. So, some extraterrestrials, if you want to call them that, draw on human emotion and take the resonance back with them to wherever they came from. Others spread love around the planet to help diminish the violent energy that humans also produce. We spirits do that too, by the way.

"Do aliens breed with humans?" I asked.

That's pretty rare. In some instances species have interbred, but mingling consciousness through DNA is only one way to share information. It can also be transmitted telepathically, just like you and I are doing right now. Remember, we're talking about energy, not physical substance. More likely, geniuses such as Einstein and Tesla are highly advanced souls who've chosen to incarnate on earth, they're not the product of human-alien inbreeding.

CHAPTER 35

On a perfect, 75-degree November day I was sitting on my back porch dressed in shorts, a T-shirt, and sandals, when a butterfly glided in for a visit. These beautiful creatures have long been linked with death and rebirth because they transform from caterpillars into butterflies. For a while it flitted around my head and shoulders, eventually landing on my upper lip. It tickled, but I resisted brushing it away--I sensed Ron was giving me a kiss.

The butterfly lingered a bit longer, then fluttered away, but a few minutes later it returned. This time it landed on the tattoo of a Celtic knot on my ankle. I laughed because that was the first place Ron kissed me.

"Are you in the butterfly or is it your messenger?" I asked.

Both. I'm in everything you see around you--and so are you.

Slowly I stretched out my leg, so I could see the butterfly's black-and-orange wings better. It hung on, unperturbed by my movement.

Don't take earth life so seriously, he told me for the umpteenth time. *A single incarnation isn't a big deal overall. Don't get so attached to it.*

Early in our relationship, Ron had impressed me by quoting passages from Shakespeare. Now I heard him recite one from *Macbeth*: *"Life's but a walking shadow, a poor player, that struts and frets his hour upon the stage, and then is heard no more; it is a tale told by an idiot, full of sound and fury, signifying nothing."*

He'd told me this before, but I had trouble seeing it from his perspective. "If that's the case, why do we invest so much effort in it?"

Why indeed? A lifetime is kind of like an athletic event. People invest so much importance in a simple ball game, but ultimately the game doesn't mean a lot-- it's soon over and all the fans go back home. Enjoy it and learn what you can in the process.

"Does that mean I can just sit out here on the back porch for the rest of my days watching butterflies?"

You could spend your time in worse ways. Actually, watching butterflies is a pretty good way to spend your time--you're being, not doing. You're peacefully in the moment. Each moment you're creating your life--this one and those in the future. Plus what you think, feel, and do each moment influences everything else in the universe. I've told you this before.

"The Butterfly Effect?"

He chuckled at my pun.

"So, while I'm just sitting here, watching butterflies, is there anything else I need to be aware of?"

Remember, but don't regret. Honor the past, but don't mourn its passing. Be at peace with the present.

The butterfly detached itself from my ankle and danced in a spiral pattern briefly, then flew away.

• • •

A few years ago, a neighbor had painted an oil portrait of Ron. He'd never liked it, but I did and I hung it on the wall above the dining table, where I could see it while I ate. When I looked at it during breakfast one morning, I thought I saw the collar of his shirt move as if he'd shrugged his shoulder just a bit.

At first I assumed my eyes were playing tricks on me, except that I'd seen similar oddities before. Not long ago, I noticed a whitish halo shimmering around Ron's head in a photo of us standing in front of the fireplace. On another occasion, in another picture, I was sure I saw a lock of his hair lift as if blown by the wind, and once he seemed to wink.

"When I look at your pictures are you looking back at me?" I asked.

Believe it, he answered. *Your eyes are playing tricks on you when you only see the surface of things, when you see in the limited, materialistic way you've been trained to see.*

I remembered the smoky orb that flew through my kitchen. I thought about the unusually brilliant light I'd seen emanating from the flowers in my friend Claire's garden. I contemplated the places Ron had shown me beyond my ordinary, everyday world.

Dr. Wayne Dyer often said, "When you change the way you look at things, the things you look at change."

275

What more might I observe if I managed to take off my blinders?

Before I'd finished my thought, I heard Ron quote William Blake: *"If the doors of perception were cleansed every thing would appear to man as it is, infinite."*

• • •

Even after all these months, I still felt fragile and less resilient than I had been before Ron went home. Little things that probably wouldn't have fazed me then now triggered a sense of helplessness. Like the morning a cup of coffee slipped from my hand and smashed on the kitchen's tile floor. A year ago I would've grumbled, maybe sworn, and then cleaned up the mess. Now I burst into tears. I identified with that shattered cup--I'd never be whole again.

Being broken open by love is a good thing, not a bad one, I heard Ron say as I began picking up the pieces and dropping them in the trash. He repeated something he'd told me before: *When you build a wall around your heart to protect yourself from perceived threats, you wall up the fear inside where it festers and feeds on itself. Better to storm the barricade and let in some light.*

I listened, but didn't reply.

Look at us, he continued. *Since I left my physical body, we've been able to deepen and expand the love between us. We're exploring a dimension in our relationship that we couldn't have gotten to before.*

"Well, I wish we could've found a less radical way to do it."

After I'd collected all the shards of china, I mopped up the spilled coffee. French roast had splattered the cabinets and appliances too, so after I finished the floor I wiped dark brown streaks that were dripping on the tile I'd just cleaned. I heard Ron chuckling behind me. Far more meticulous than I could ever be, he would never have made such a mess--and I was sure he didn't have to bother with such things where he lived now.

As I set about brewing another pot of coffee, Ron said, *When you "fall in love" you open the door to your heart and let the love that's already in there rush out to greet the other person. What's more, you see that person as he or she really is--a being made of love, by love. Usually people think that loving means focusing your affection on someone or something, but actually love exists in and of itself--you don't need an object to inspire it.*

"Why didn't we understand that while you were still human?" I lamented.

I don't know, baby. We would've been a whole lot happier. Remember, though, you always have the choice to experience love or hide from it. You don't have to wait for someone to come along and light your fire, and you don't have to be joyless the rest of your life. You can live love anytime you want to--preferably all the time. It's your natural state of being. We're born loving. We learn fear later.

I poured myself a fresh cup of coffee and sat at the dining table, where I could look at Ron's portrait while he talked to me. This time the subject in the painting didn't move, or perhaps I just didn't notice it.

When you feel pain--physical or emotional--it's a sign that you're losing energy, he explained. *Holes form in your energy field. You're like a tire with a puncture, losing air. When you lose energy you get sick. When you realign yourself with love and come back into harmony you heal. That's why "miraculous" cures happen sometimes. People plug back into the primal life force and that ramps up their vitality.*

For several months I'd been troubled by pain in the lower part of my back, near what yogis and holistic healers call the root chakra, located at the base of the spine. This energy center relates to a person's sense of security. Although I'd blamed the problem on a horseback riding incident, I knew that wasn't the whole truth.

In her book *Awakening Intuition,* Mona Lisa Schultz, MD, PhD, writes that lower back pain often occurs in people who are experiencing difficulties related to their marriages or primary partnerships. When viewed from these perspectives, the back pain clearly reflected my situation. I'd always thought of Ron as my safe harbor, my knight in shining armor, the person I relied on for direction and protection. Without him I felt scared and insecure, adrift in a turbulent sea without a compass. No wonder my lower back hurt.

When I was human, I was your port in the storm and you were my light in the darkness. That hasn't changed since I came home. As I've said before, I can take better care of you now than I could when I was in a physical body. Remember when you were driving last week and swerved to miss hitting a squirrel?

The near-accident popped up on my mental screen. I was driving about 60 mph when a squirrel suddenly darted in front of my car. Instinctively, I jerked the wheel sharply to the right to avoid hitting the animal, a move my top-heavy SUV didn't handle very well. Just as I realized the vehicle might roll, I felt a hand grab the steering wheel and correct my trajectory.

"You did that," I said.

Of course. Somebody has to watch out for you. I'm there, taking care of you during storms too.

In the Texas Hill Country, ferocious thunderstorms lashed the countryside, downing trees and whipping up flash floods. They terrified me and I cowered when lightning bolts exploded around my hilltop home. How much of my life did Ron and other benevolent spirits guide? Did they oversee all those everyday events I muddled through?

Yesterday, when you were walking barefoot in the bedroom, you heard me yell "Stop" right before you would've stepped on a scorpion. I've got your back, baby. Really, you don't need to feel insecure about anything.

As I finished the last of my coffee, I heard him singing Beyoncé's "Trust in Me."

• • •

That evening, I sat down to read a book by Sirona Knight titled *Love, Sex, and Magick.* As often happened, the book fell open to a page that held special meaning for me. It said: "Love is the light in which we see each thing in its true origin, image, nature, and destiny. Unless you see someone or something in the light of love, you do not see them or it at all."

CHAPTER 36

For those of us who have lost loved ones, the holiday season between Thanksgiving and New Year's is probably the worst time of the year. The emphasis on enjoying time with the people who are precious to us exacerbates the loneliness we endure. The spate of festivities rubs our noses in the joylessness of our empty lives.

Christmas, however, never mattered much to me. Ron and I weren't religious. Neither of us had children, and our few family members lived far enough away that we rarely saw each other. To tell the truth, I felt relieved that I didn't have to attend perfunctory holiday get-togethers with people I didn't like or crawl the malls buying gifts for relatives and friends who didn't need anything. Usually, Ron and I marked the holiday modestly by cooking a special meal together and sharing it with an expensive bottle of wine in front of the fireplace. We didn't decorate a tree, exchange presents, or watch sentimental old movies on TV. In this part of Texas, it didn't even snow.

So I was surprised at how out of sorts I felt as the holiday approached. On Christmas morning, reluctant to face the day, I lay in bed until almost eleven o'clock, snuggled in my down comforter, drifting in and out of sleep.

Finally, I got up to feed Zoe, took a long shower, and made breakfast. While coffee brewed, I prepared a western omelet for myself and warmed up some cornbread.

Stop feeling sorry for yourself, I heard Ron say.

"Aren't I entitled to feel sad?" I asked, sipping my coffee. "It's Christmas and the love of my life is dead and I'm all alone in the world."

A noise that sounded very much like a raspberry buzzed in my ears.

Self-pity, he said. *How many times do I have to tell you that you're not alone? Right now ten beings, including me, are sitting right here at this table with you. Besides, while you're bemoaning your sorry state of affairs, people all over the world are starving, suffering from horrible illnesses, and killing each other in stupid battles. You are one of the most fortunate women on the entire planet. You have good health, intelligence, talent, friends, a comfortable home, and so much more. Do you have any idea how many people didn't eat today? How many don't have roofs over their heads? Be grateful, Skye.*

I bit into my cornbread and rested my elbows on the oak table. "What does my sadness have to do with any of them? I can't change their situations."

Everything, he answered. *First of all, the longer you focus on what you lack, the longer you'll experience lack in your life. Second, all that sadness you send out into the world adds to the huge repository of misery that's already saturating earth. Your job is to bring love and light to the planet, not to make things worse.*

I plunged my fork into the omelet. Salsa oozed out of the yellow pocket and spread, blood-like, across the plate. I laid the fork down and dissolved into tears.

"I can't do this, Ron. I can't keep going on with this sham. I've tried--you know I've tried--but it's no use. Without you, nothing matters. I just want to die and be there with you."

I felt him patiently stroking my head while I cried myself out. When I finally stopped sobbing, he said, *Eat your breakfast, then I have a present for you.*

Like an obedient child, I shoveled food into my mouth and chewed, barely tasting it. I sipped my coffee. When I'd finished, I crossed my knife and fork on the plate and folded my napkin.

"Who else is here with you?" I wished I could see the spirits he'd said were in the room too. Most of all I wished I could see Ron.

Grace, Kailleagh, Megan and Moriah. Your grandmother. Your friend Jocelyn. The rest you knew in other lifetimes.

All together they began singing: *We wish you a merry Christmas . . . and a happy New Year.* The clarity of their voices and the intricate harmonies they wove together transformed the simple carol into an exquisite choral tapestry. Above the other voices I heard Ron's--

not the voice he'd spoken with while embodied, yet I knew it was his, and the shimmering, bell-like tone filled me with awe.

When the song ended, I asked, "Is this what the heavenly choir sounds like?"

Ron laughed. *One way we communicate over here is by singing--harmonic resonance is the language of spirits. That's why I can sing to you now, even though I could barely squawk out a note when I was human.*

For a while longer, the group continued singing familiar songs and ones I'd never heard before, some in a language I couldn't understand, each more beautiful than the last. The music not only filled the room, it filled me as well. The sadness that had gripped me earlier dissolved.

"What a lovely gift," I said. "Thank you."

CHAPTER 37

On the afternoon of March 17, 2014, eleven months and thirteen days after Ron went home, I sat on my back porch as I often did at the end of the day. The wide-open space, big sky, and quiet that I'd found unnerving when I first moved to Texas in 2005 now soothed me, and I never tired of watching the deer, antelope, jackrabbits, birds, and other wildlife.

Despite my Irish lineage and my thirty-one years living in the Boston area, I didn't celebrate St. Patrick's Day, which marks the ascent of Christianity in the Emerald Isle and its assault on the indigenous pagan culture. Ron, the son of a defrocked Catholic priest from Donnegal, also ignored what we both considered a much overrated and misunderstood holiday.

I don't believe in coincidences, but I still don't know why he chose that particular day.

As I sat overlooking the eastern part of my property on that salubrious sunny afternoon, I spotted a man standing in a clearing at the bottom of the hill, perhaps two hundred feet away, facing in my direction. I hadn't noticed him only a moment ago--he seemed to have appeared out of nowhere. Where had he come from?

He had white hair, but from this distance I couldn't make out his facial features. What surprised me was he wore only a pair of black shorts. I'd never seen anyone walking shirtless around our ranch--even in April the scalding Texas sun can cause sunburn or skin cancer, especially in light-skinned Caucasians like the man at the bottom of the hill.

While I watched, he started walking along the road that bordered my property. After a couple minutes, he turned and began climbing the hill toward my house. Startled, I wondered why a stranger would head up this rocky incline, dodging prickly vegetation, not to mention fire ants, snakes, scorpions, and other creepy-crawlies. What could he possible want?

Anxiety flickered in my stomach.

The man stopped, turned around, and made his way back through the cactus and agarita to the road, where he continued walking for another minute or so. He passed a neighbor with his dog, but they didn't exchange greetings, as would normally have occurred in this friendly community. How strange, I thought.

Once again, the white-haired man left the road and started trudging up the rocky hill toward my house. Then just as suddenly as he'd appeared, he vanished.

Where had he gone? My view to the road was unobstructed. No big live oaks or cedar trees stood in the man's path. He couldn't have ducked down behind a clump of paddle cactus--I'd watched his every step. My senses shifted into high alert.

As my mind struggled to make sense of what I'd seen, I heard Ron's voice. *Don't you recognize me?*

"Oh my god," I blurted out. "It's really you? You're here?"

I didn't mean to scare you.

"Well, I wasn't exactly expecting to see you."

I'm glad you finally did. It's really hard to maintain that level of density for such a long time. You need a lot of skill and concentration to move naturally when you don't have a physical body. Otherwise you end up looking like a zombie.

I paced back and forth on my porch, folding and unfolding my arms. Thoughts tumbled around in my addled mind. Is this for real? I kept asking myself.

During the past year I'd come to accept and depend on Ron's daily communications from the other side. Seeing him, however--not as a wispy ghost, but looking as solid as he'd been in physical life--defied comprehension. Could I believe what I'd seen? Maybe I had imagined the whole experience. Had the grief and upset of the past year completely undone my sense of reality?

"How did you manage to make yourself look as if you were flesh and blood?" I asked.

By focusing my energy and projecting that image to you, he answered. *I showed you an illusion, like a holograph. What people see on earth is a shared illusion--an agreed upon standard of what exists, what they've been conditioned to accept. Not what's real. Nothing's really solid, you know. All material things are made up of moving molecules with a whole lot of space in between. You only see what you're prepared to see. I could have paraded around for days in the supermarket and no one would've noticed me. But you did, because you were open to the possibility, even though it startled you when it happened.*

"That's amazing! It makes me think of when Jesus showed himself to his followers after the Crucifixion to let them know that life continues after death. A lot of people thought they saw a physical human being, but he wasn't corporeal--he could walk through walls."

Ron laughed. *Well, I'm no Jesus as you know, but I can walk through walls too.*

"I guess if you don't have to lug around a clunky body, you can do stuff like that. Thanks for showing up, darlin'. Even though you startled me."

That Ron had suffered the fatal stroke on Good Friday and gone home four days later also struck me as meaningful. I didn't compare Ron to Jesus, and yet the message the great avatar brought us--that we are all eternal and earthly incarnation is only a step along the journey--seemed in line with what Ron was trying to explain to me.

That evening I phoned my friend Lyndsey to tell her what had happened. Although most people would have considered me crazy, she didn't.

"Here's something else to think about," she said, after I'd finished pouring out my account. "In Carlos Castenada's books he writes about shamans who could energetically project their images over great distances, so people in various places would see them as if they were really there in the flesh."

"That's pretty much how Ron explained what he did."

"Girl, you are on to something."

"What?"

"I'm not sure, but I don't know anyone else who's seen a fully formed, solid-looking apparition. We've all heard about creaking floorboards, things that go bump in the night, and rocking chairs with no one in them. And ghosts, like the ones at Claire's house. But nothing like what you described."

In the days that followed, as I replayed the memory of Ron's unexpected appearance from the other side, I realized I didn't know what he'd worn the day he had the fatal stroke. I wasn't with him when the artery in his brain burst, and by the time I got to the hospital he was dressed in a johnnie.

Curious, I contacted the neighbor who'd responded to Ron's 911 call. He told me when he'd arrived, Ron had on only a pair of black gym shorts.

• • •

Five weeks later I saw Ron again, walking down the road below my house just as he had before. This time, however, he only appeared for a minute or so. After his image faded, I sensed he probably wouldn't show himself to me that way again--nor did I need him to. I knew he was every bit as alive and present as he'd been when he was human--more so, in fact--and that he would be with me always.

• • •

Years after my beloved Ron Conroy went home, and after a great deal of soul-searching--along with help from many generous beings on the other side--I've come to understand a few things about the afterlife and about life on earth that I might never have realized had I not been forced to look at what we call "death" squarely in the face.

For me, the most important of these revelations is that love never dies. It can't, just as energy can't be destroyed. Love is the inimitable, omnipotent, and all-encompassing force that creates and perpetuates the world we know as well as the infinite worlds beyond. We are made of and by love--even if we sometimes feel unloving or unlovable. We're drawn together by love and we're held together by love. We can't be parted from those we love. Our loved ones, who now live on the other side, are never more than a heartbeat away. We can communicate with them, sense their presence, even see them if we choose. Contact with loving spirits in other levels of reality isn't the exclusive province of psychics, mediums, or mystics. Anyone can interact with beings who no longer occupy bodies made of flesh and blood. The only requirements are an open mind and an open heart.

We are all eternal. As souls, we are indestructible. We shed our physical forms, the way snakes shed their old skins, in order to keep growing. The snake doesn't die when it sloughs off its too-tight skin and we don't die when we leave the bodies that have served us well during our sojourn on earth.

After we've accomplished what we came here to do, we simply move on. We continue living wherever and in whatever manner suits our purposes. We walk through the revolving doors again and again, always curious and eager to discover what lies on the other side.

In the words of the Chinese Taoist thinker Chuang Tzu, "Birth is not a beginning; death is not an end."

It's that simple, and that wondrous.

About the Author

Skye Alexander is the author of more than forty fiction and nonfiction books, many on metaphysical subjects. She is a frequent guest on radio shows and podcasts, and has been interviewed by media including CNN, *USA Today*, *Better Homes and Gardens*, *Cosmopolitan*, and *Playboy*. The BBC filmed her with Ron at Stonehenge for a Discovery Channel TV special, titled "Secret Stonehenge." After living in Massachusetts for thirty-one years, she now makes her home in Texas with her black Manx cat Zoe.

Visit her at www.skyealexander.com.

CPSIA information can be obtained
at www.ICGtesting.com
Printed in the USA
LVHW050313110222
710655LV00003B/442

9 781647 198329